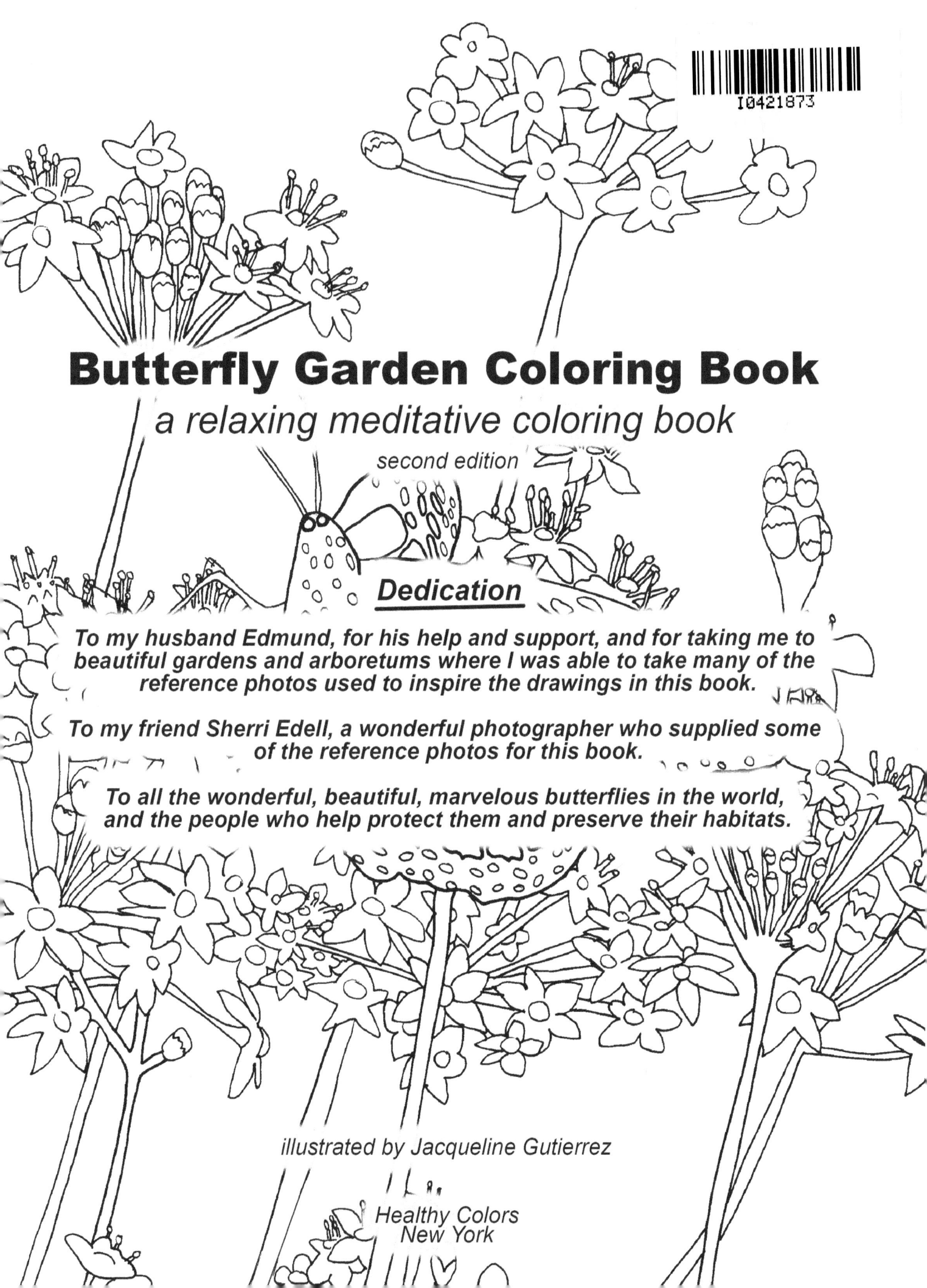

Butterfly Garden Coloring Book

a relaxing meditative coloring book

second edition

Dedication

To my husband Edmund, for his help and support, and for taking me to beautiful gardens and arboretums where I was able to take many of the reference photos used to inspire the drawings in this book.

To my friend Sherri Edell, a wonderful photographer who supplied some of the reference photos for this book.

To all the wonderful, beautiful, marvelous butterflies in the world, and the people who help protect them and preserve their habitats.

illustrated by Jacqueline Gutierrez

Healthy Colors
New York

Butterflies

This book was inspired by the beauty of the butterfly.

I was lucky enough to have seen many of these butterflies in person, and took many of the reference photos myself that inspired the creation of this book.

Butterflies are free to fly, and do so beautifully and gracefully.

I hope that you enjoy coloring these butterflies as much as I enjoyed drawing them.

Butterflies need your protection. Avoid using pesticides which can harm butterflies. Plant native flowers that provide nectar for the butterflies, such as Butterfly bush, Echinacea, Milkweed, and Zinnias.

Butterfly Garden Coloring Book, a relaxing meditative coloring book
illustrated by Jacqueline Gutierrez

Published by:
Healthy Colors, *an imprint of Sprouting Seed Press*
690 Saratoga Road, Suite 183, Burnt Hills, NY 12027
http://www.healthycolors.com, http://www.sproutingseedpress.com

Second edition

ISBN-13:978-0996835503
ISBN-10:0996835504

Reference photos from:
Jacqueline S. Gutierrez
Sherri D. Edell
Adobe Stock

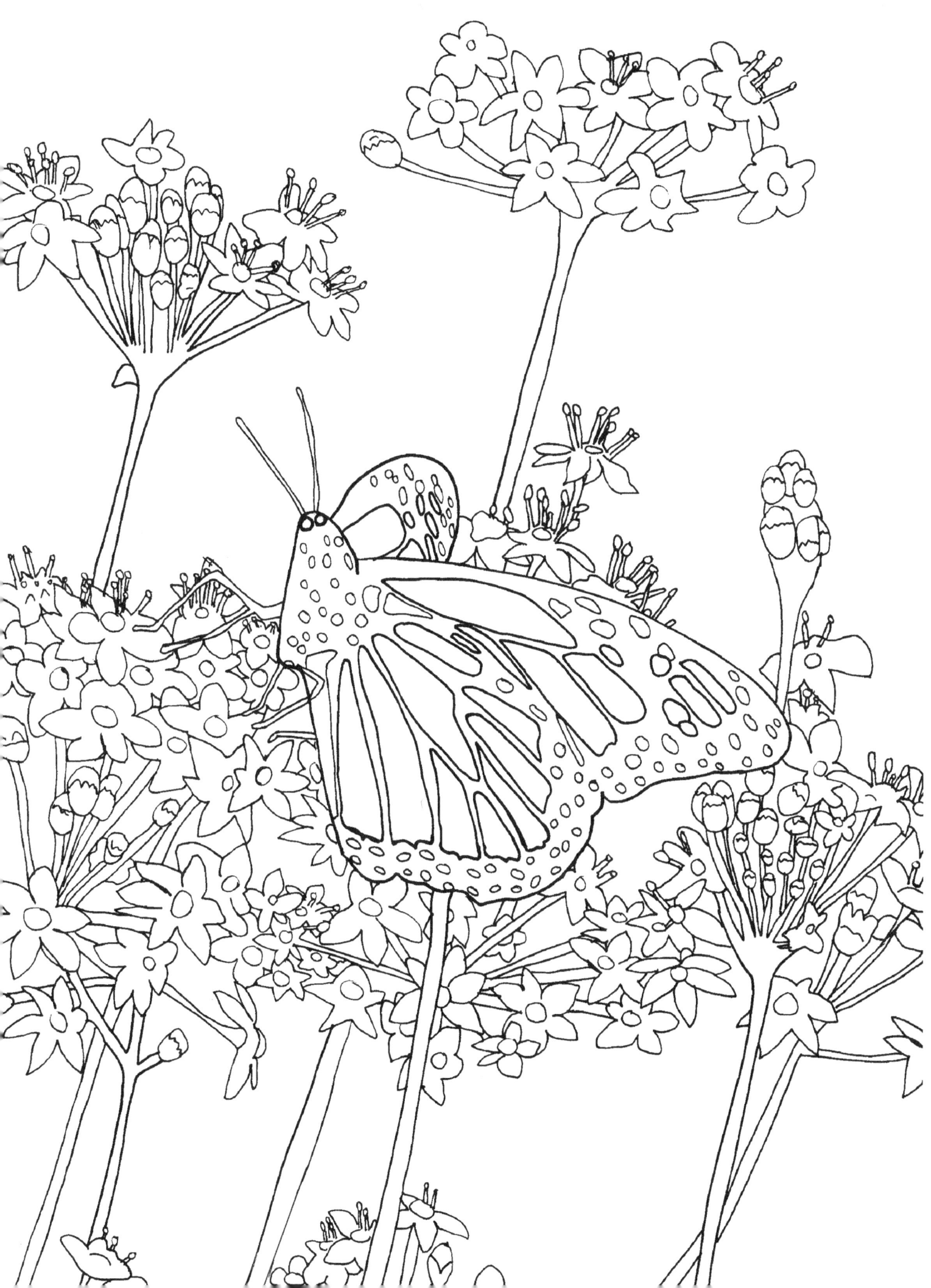

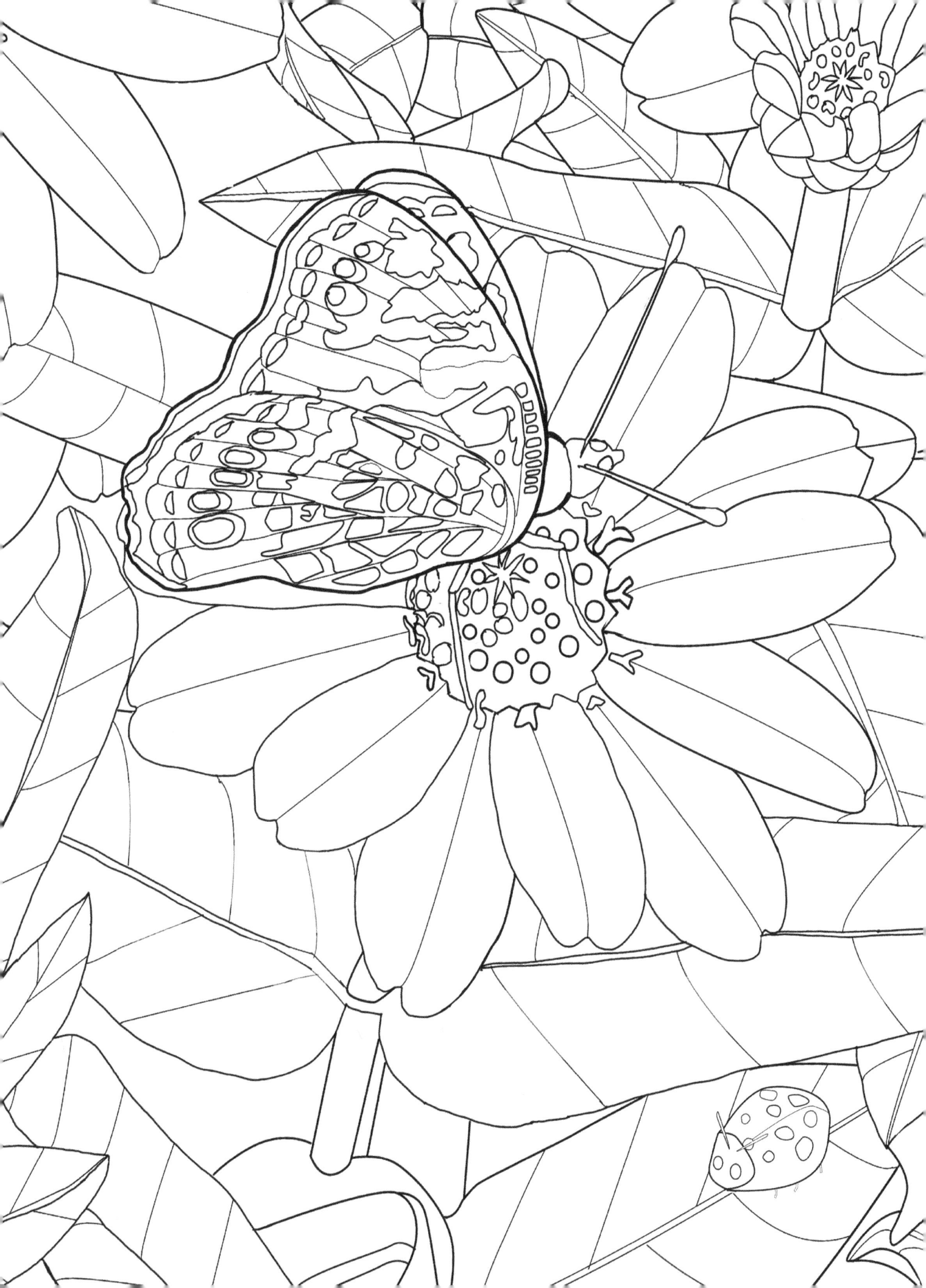

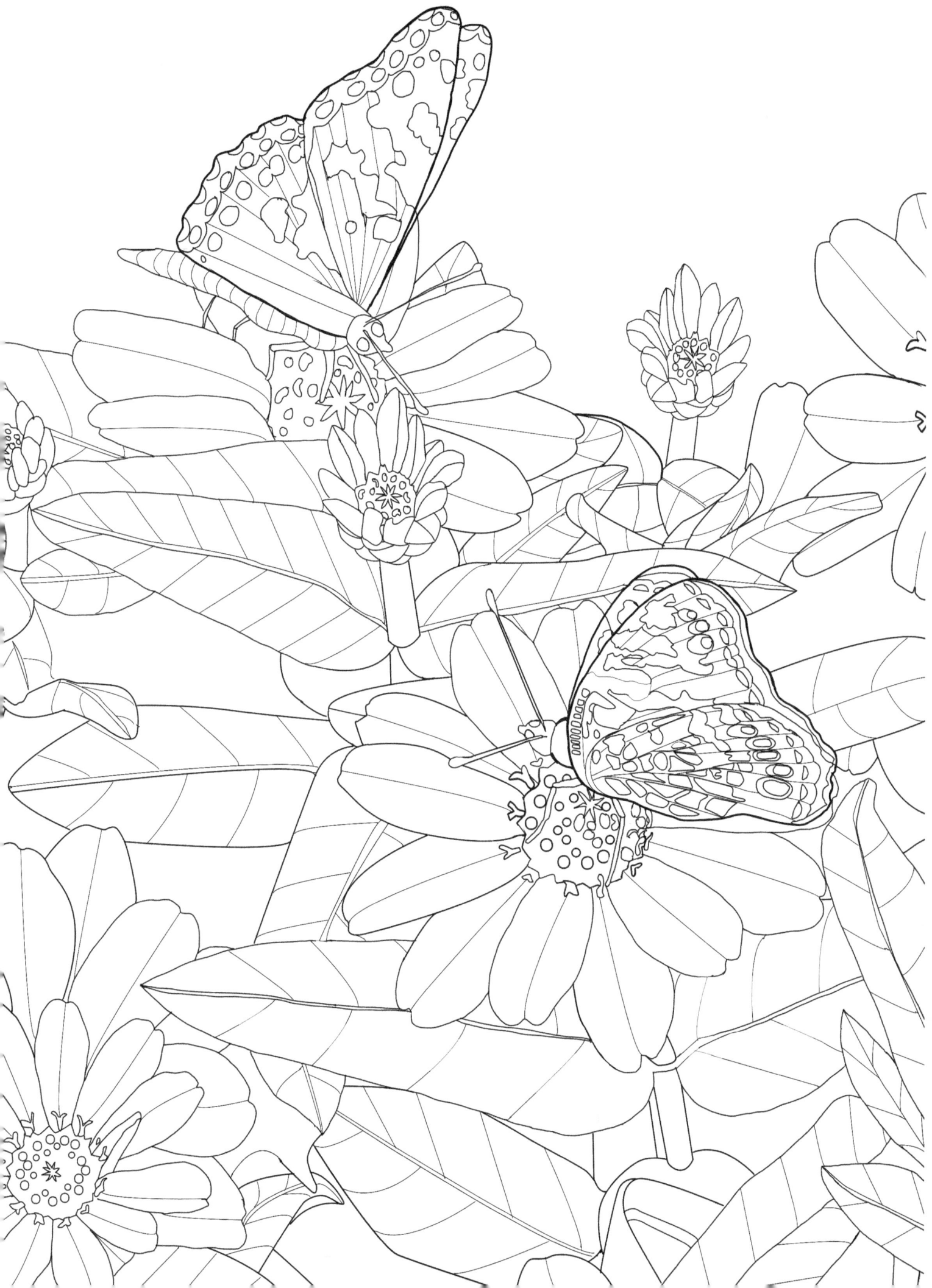

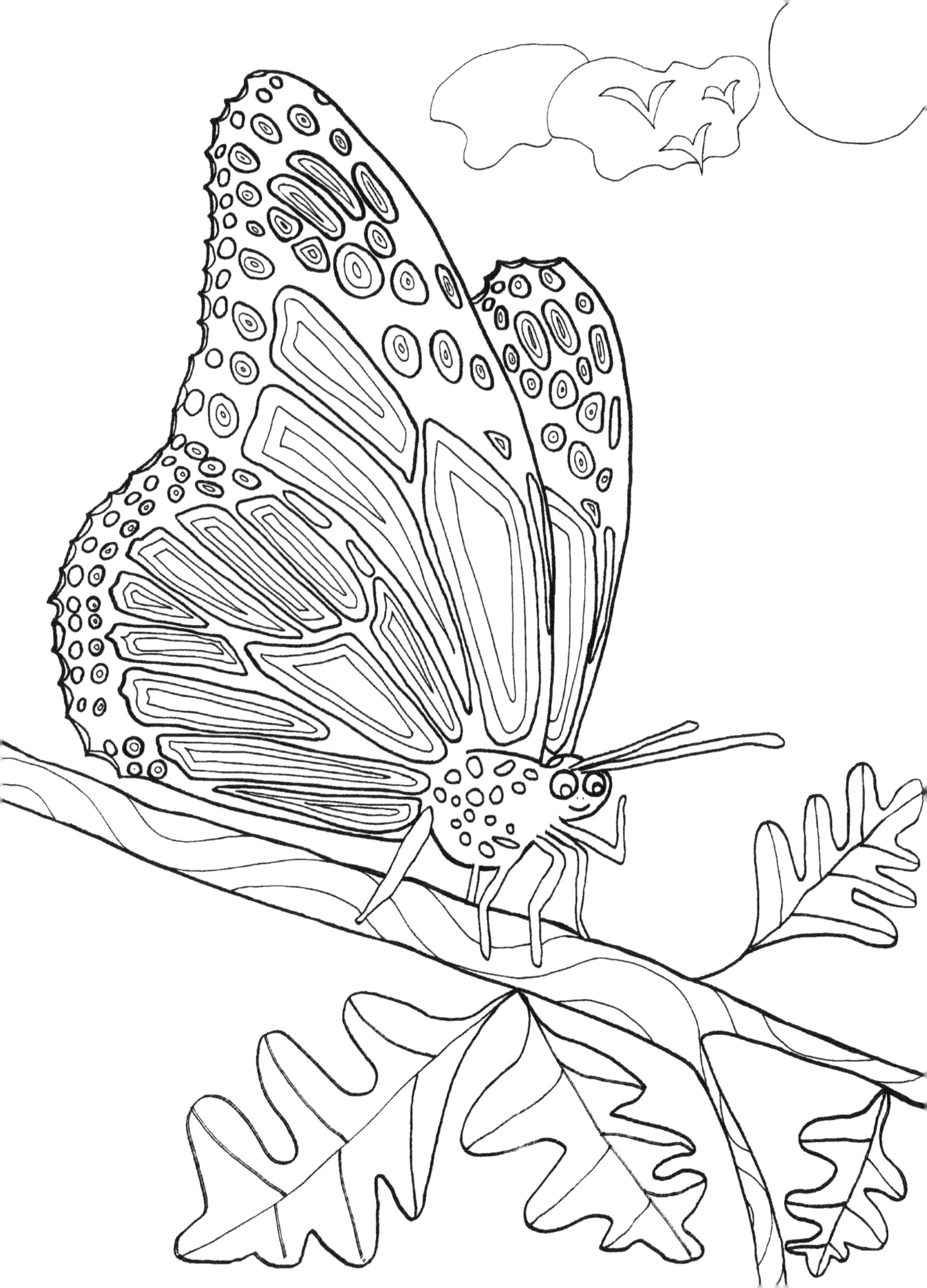

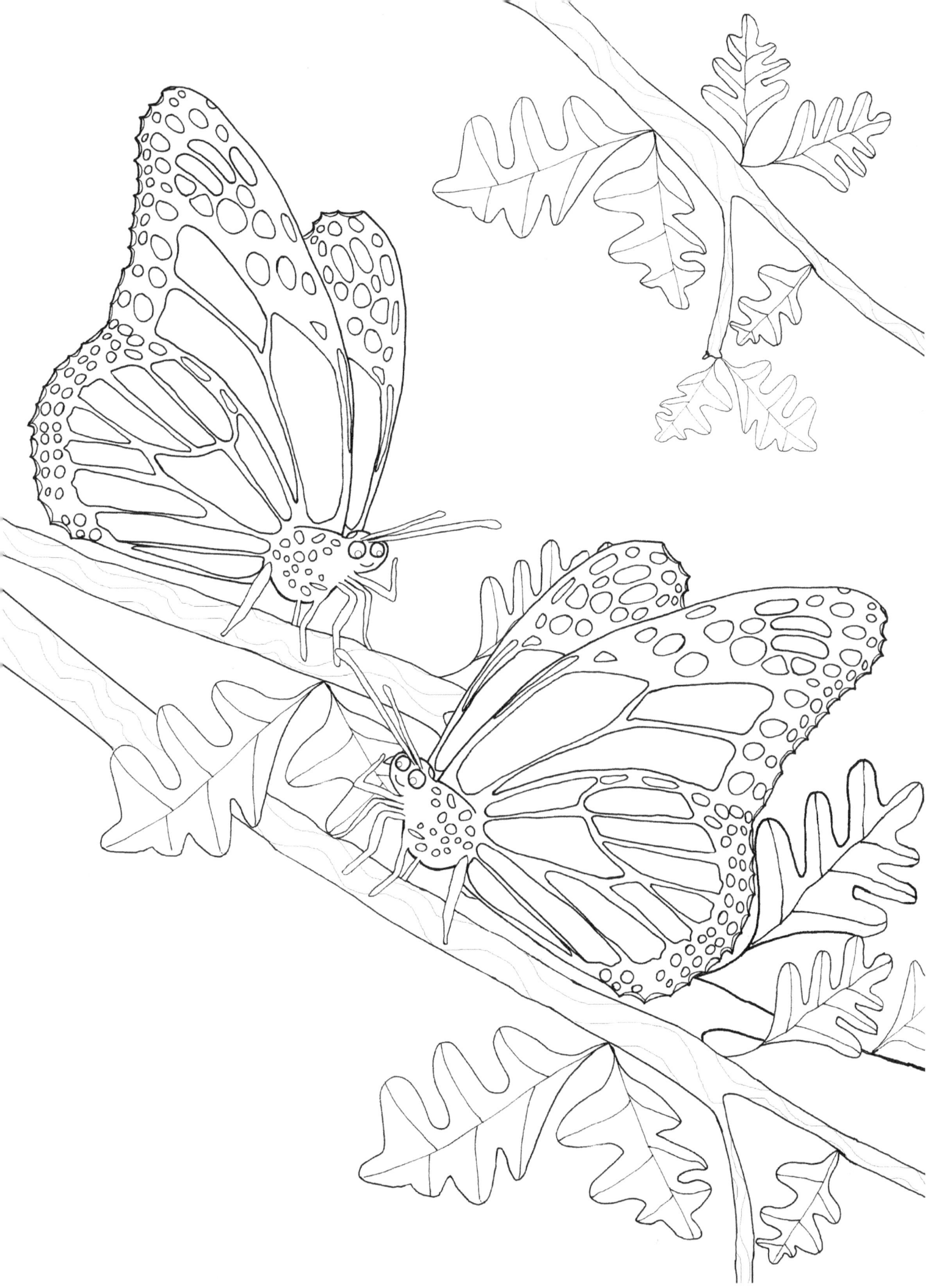

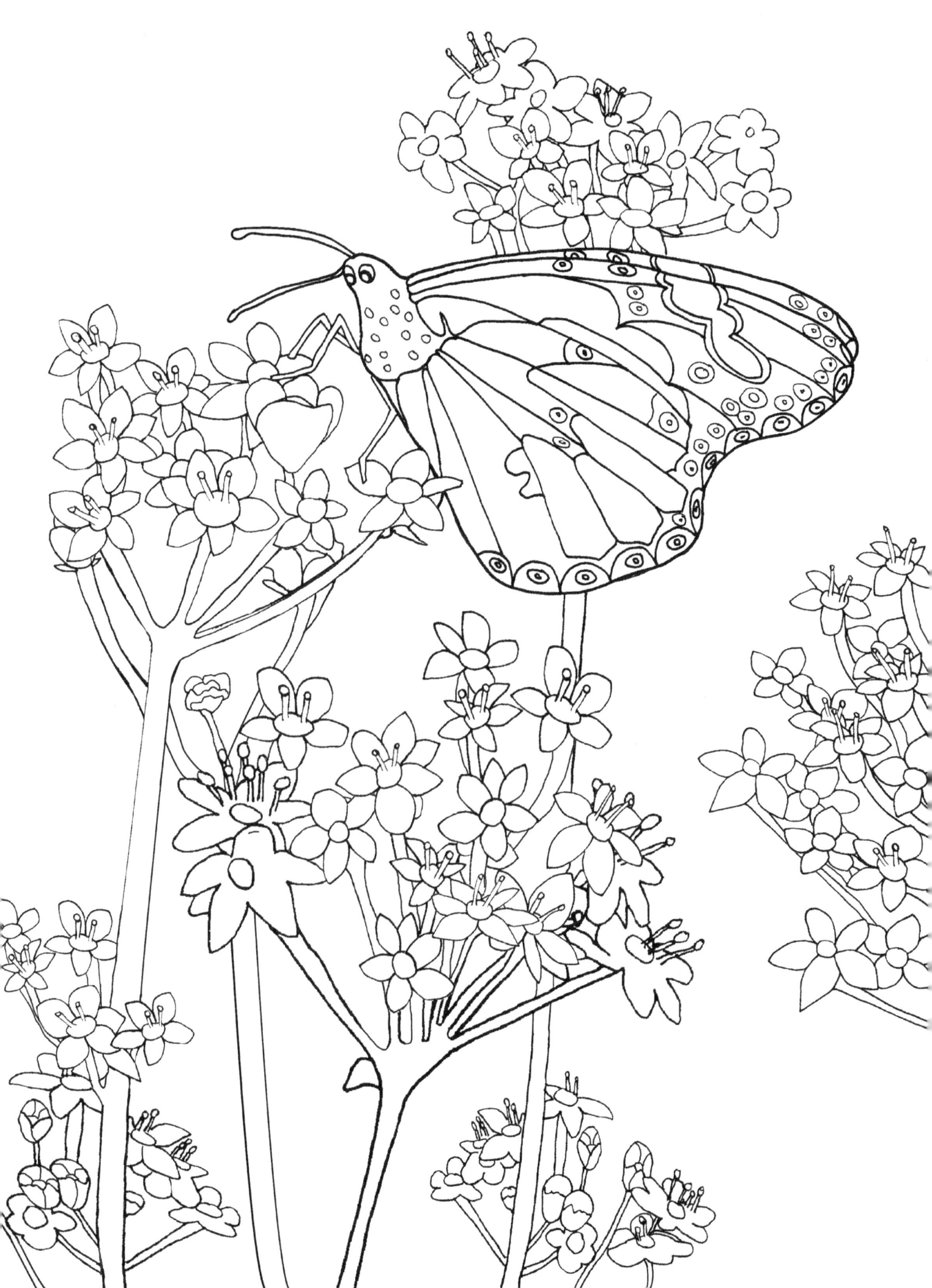

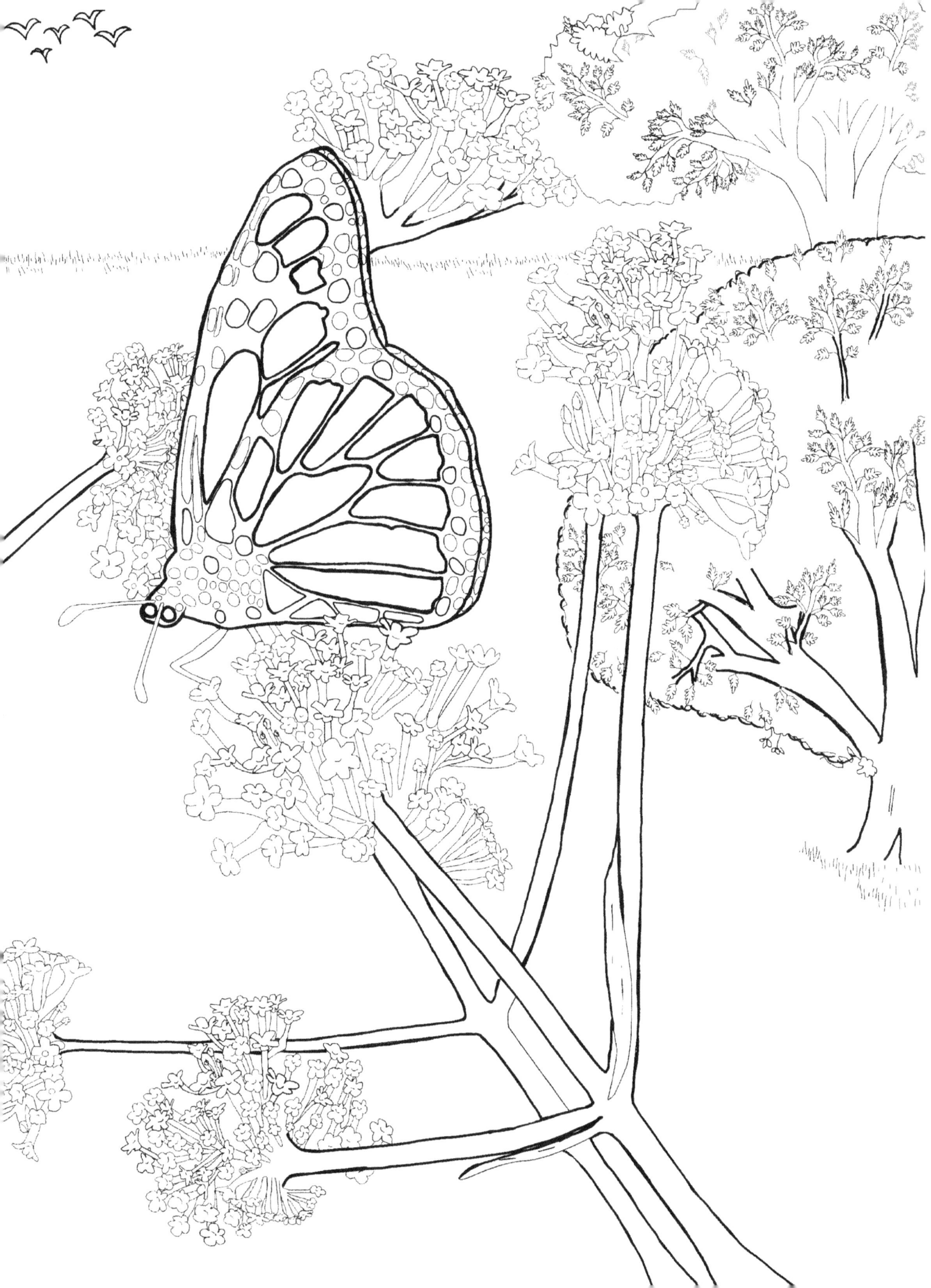

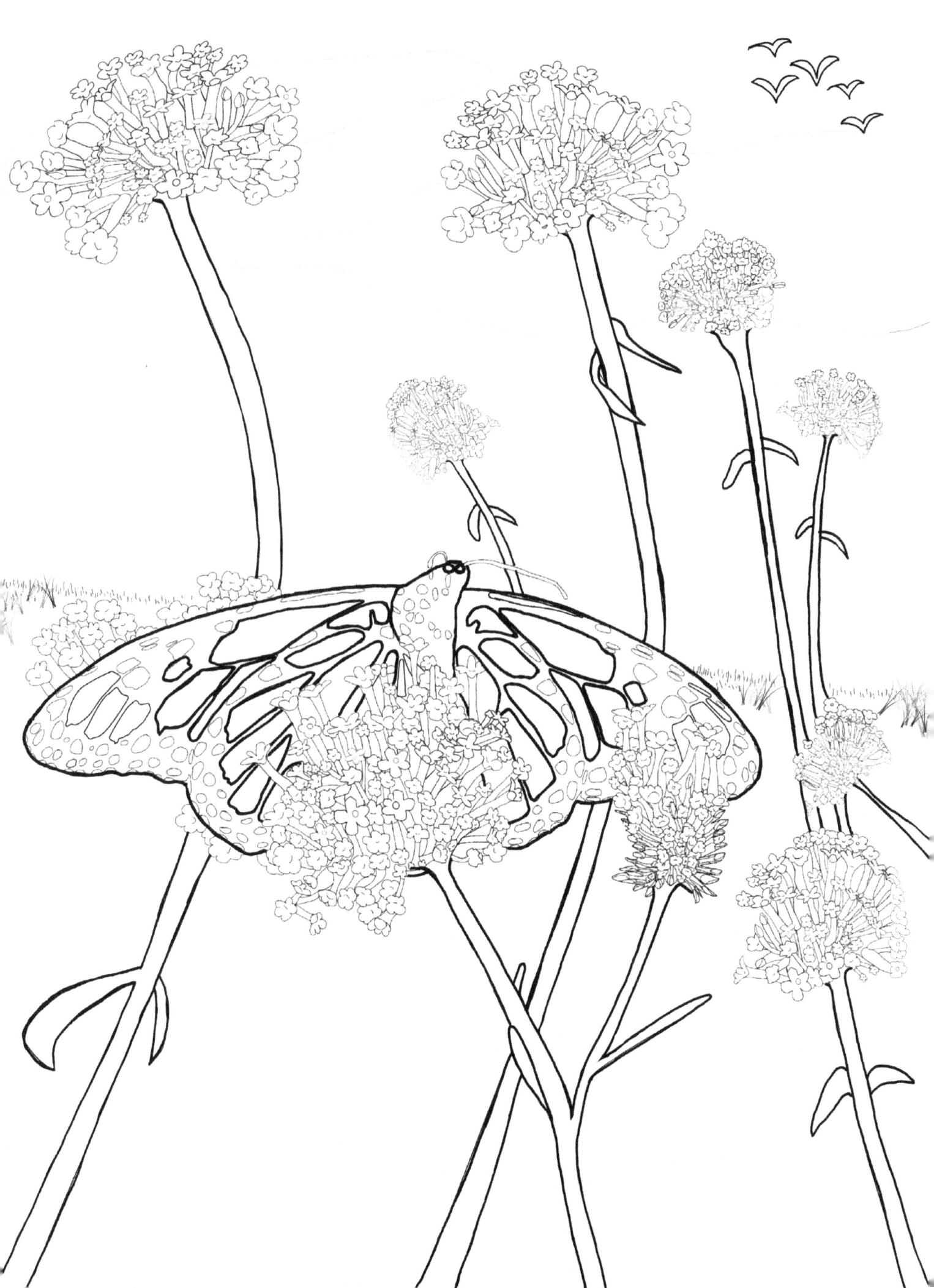

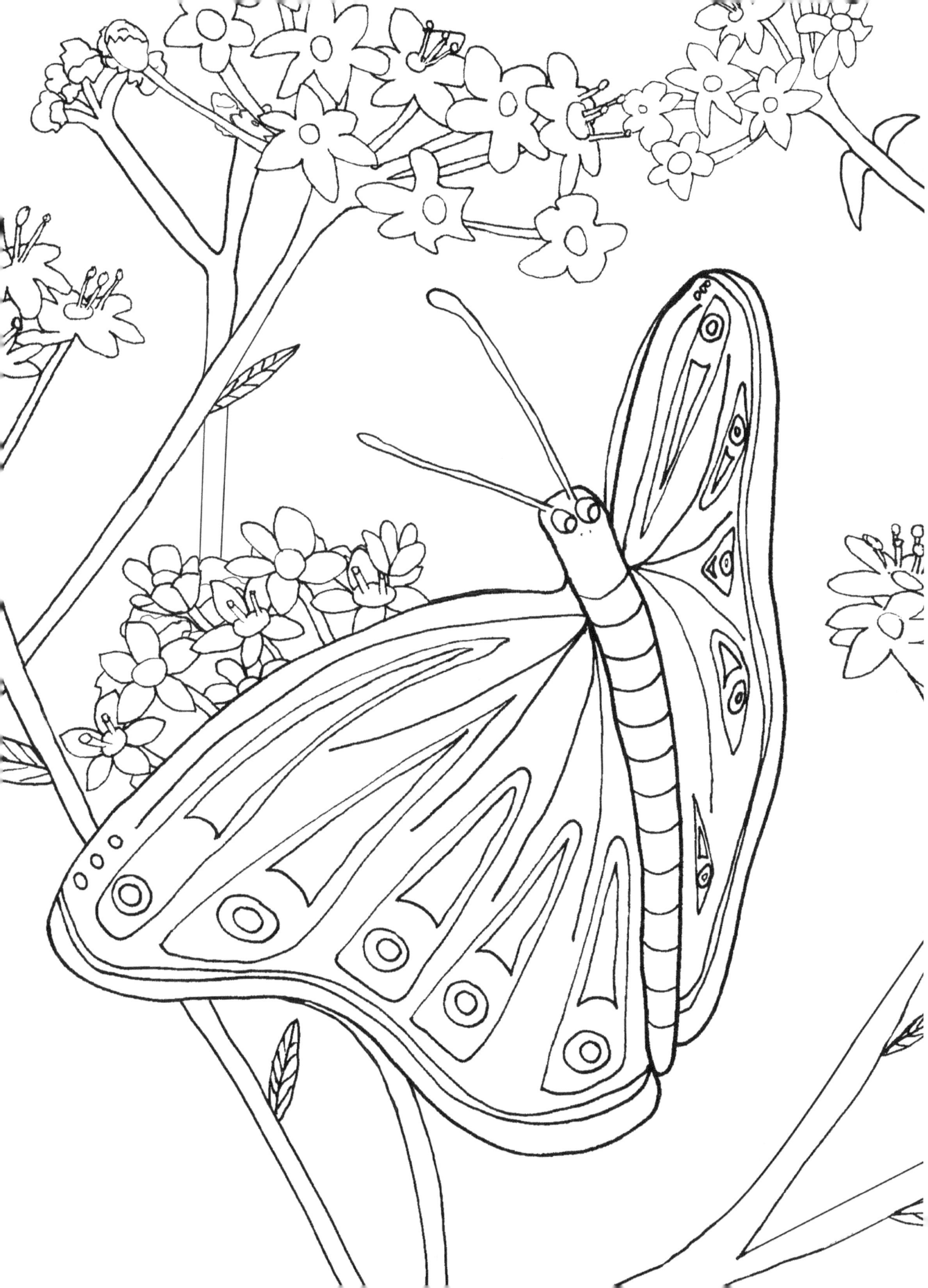

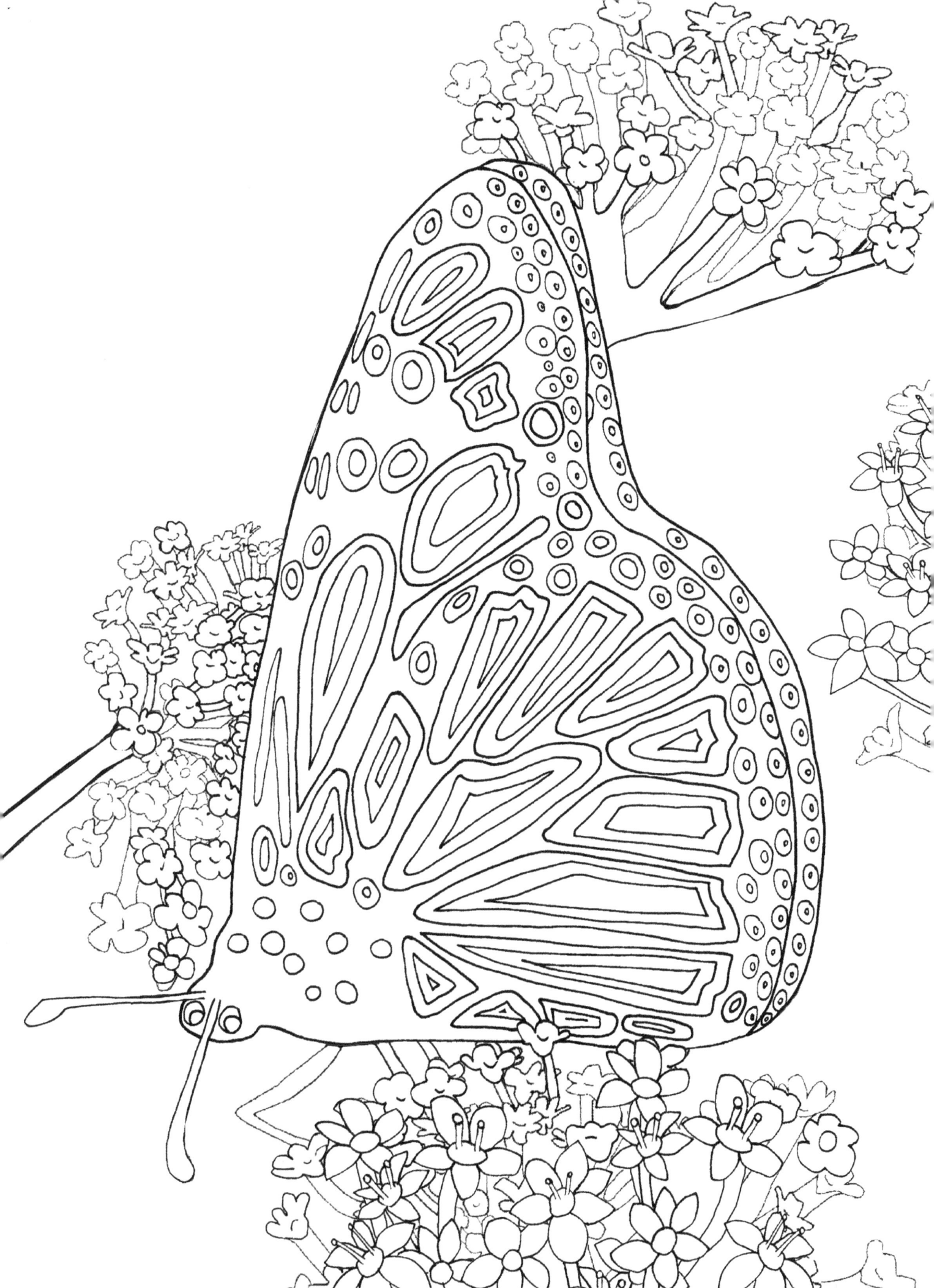

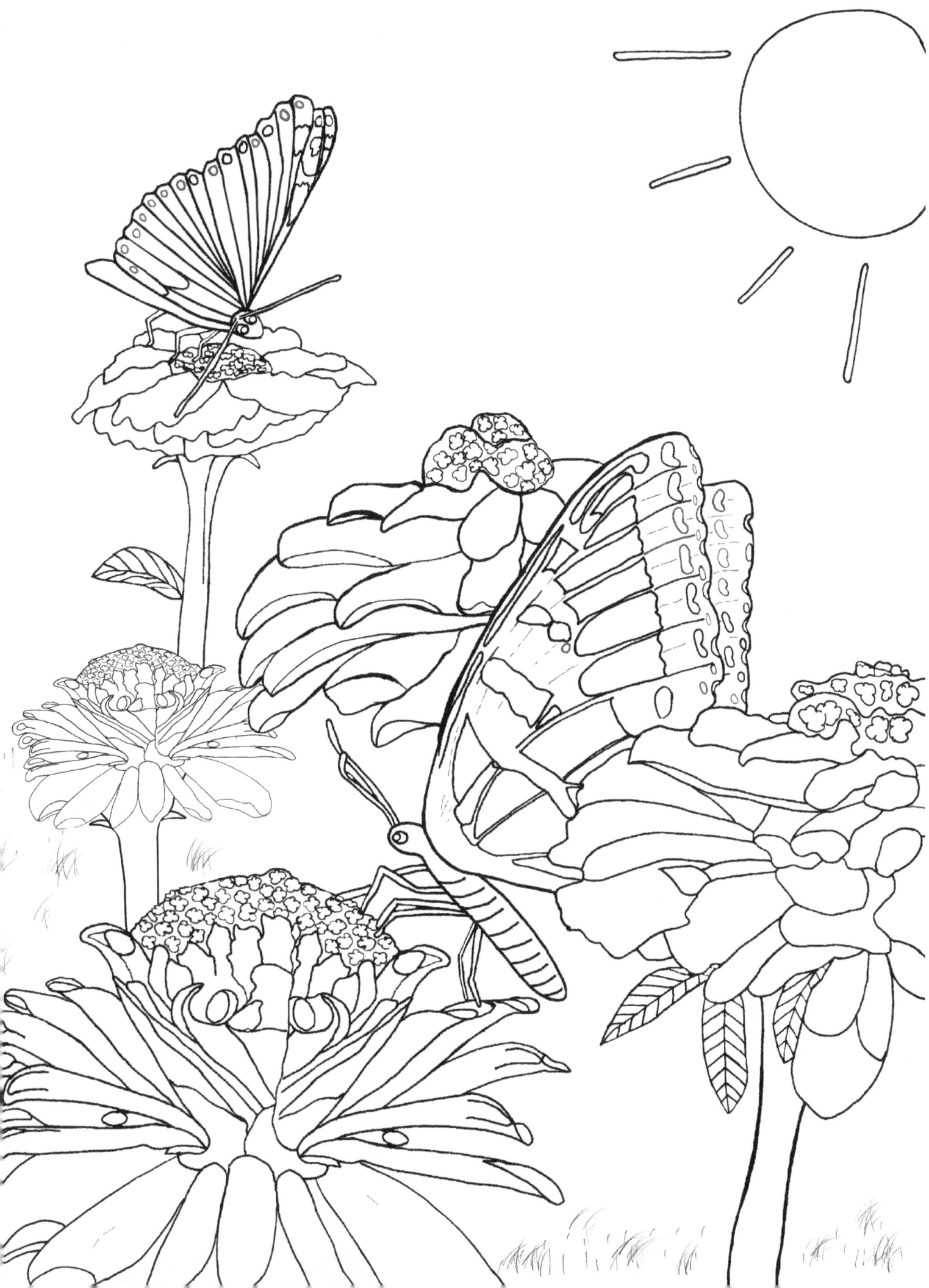

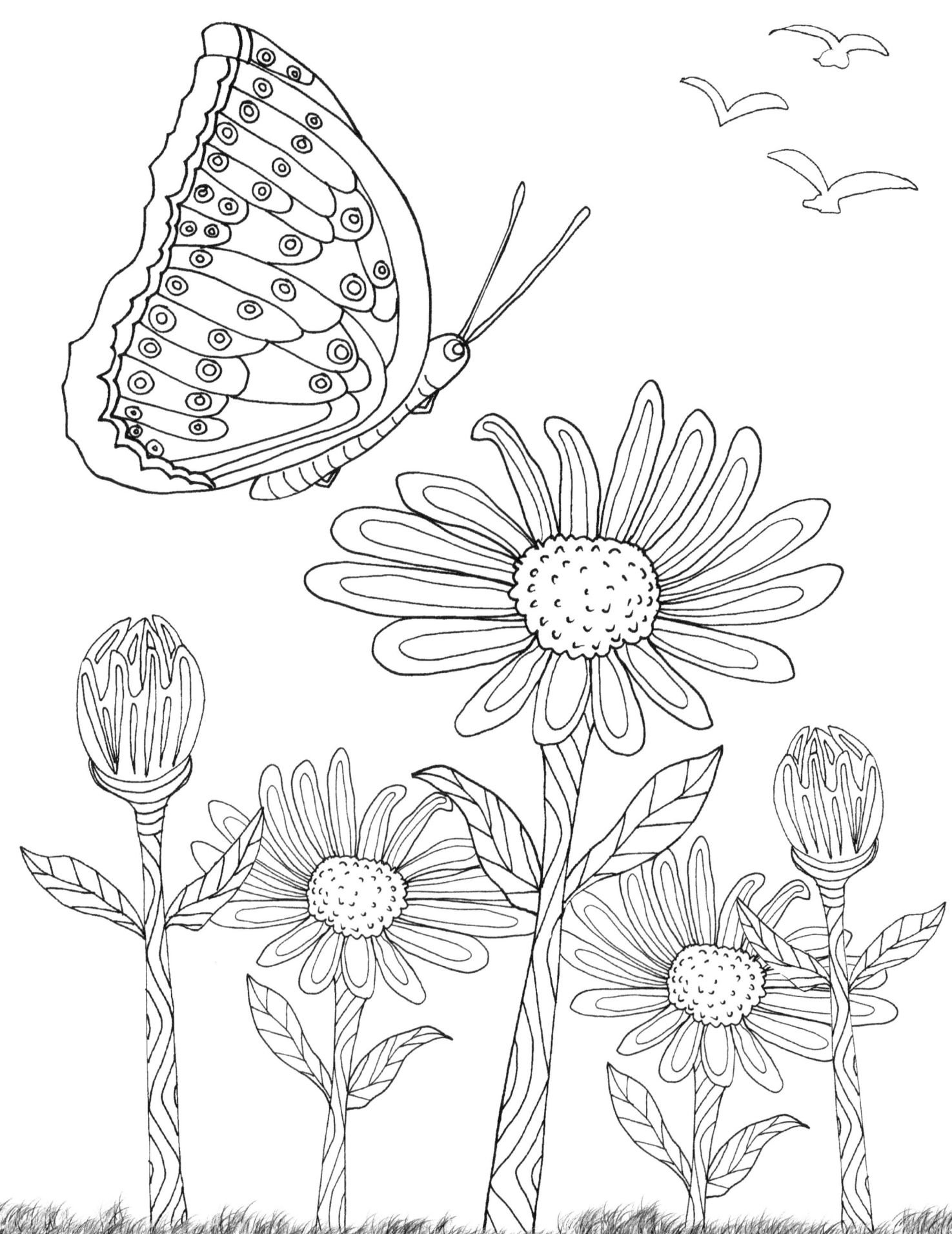

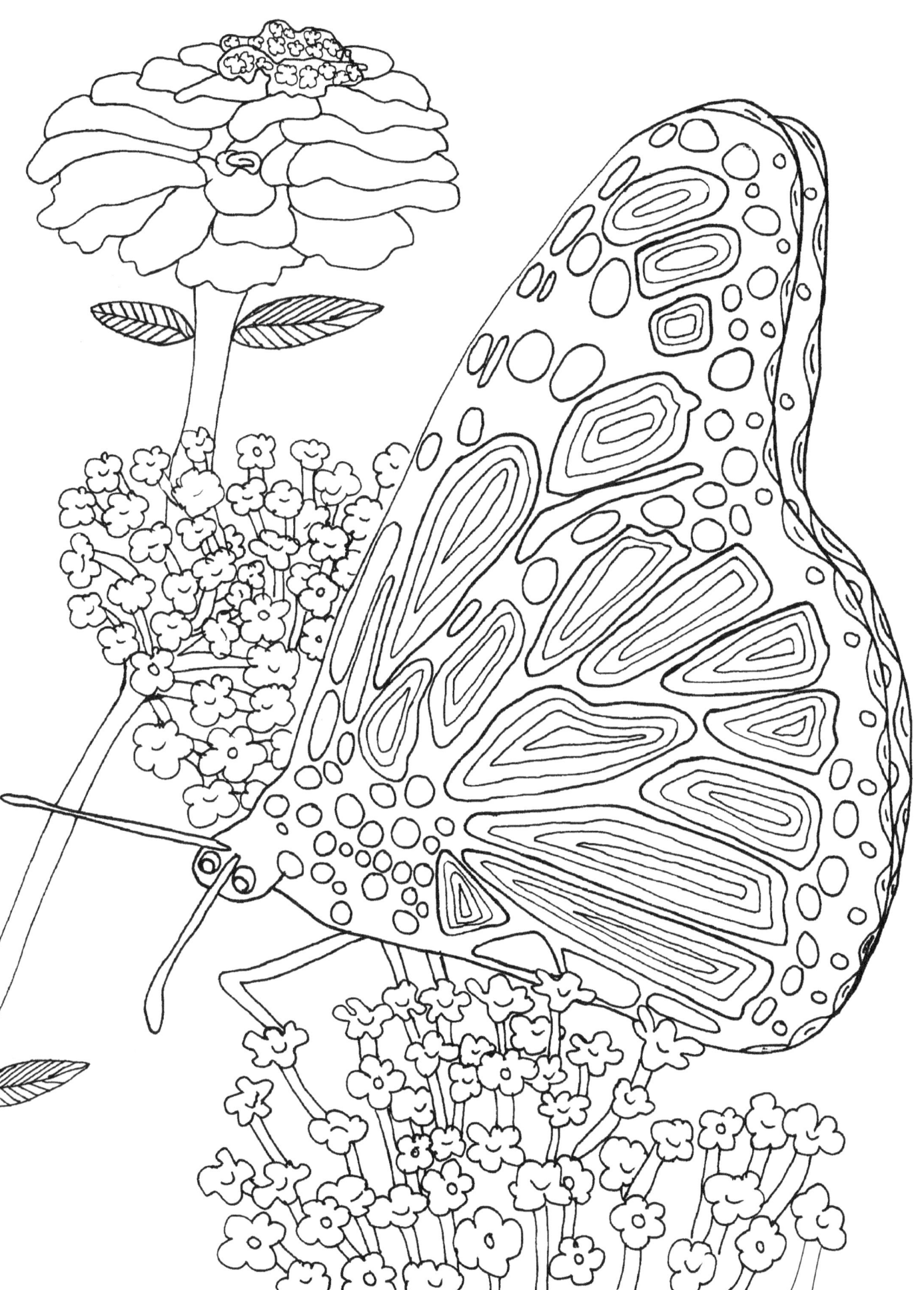

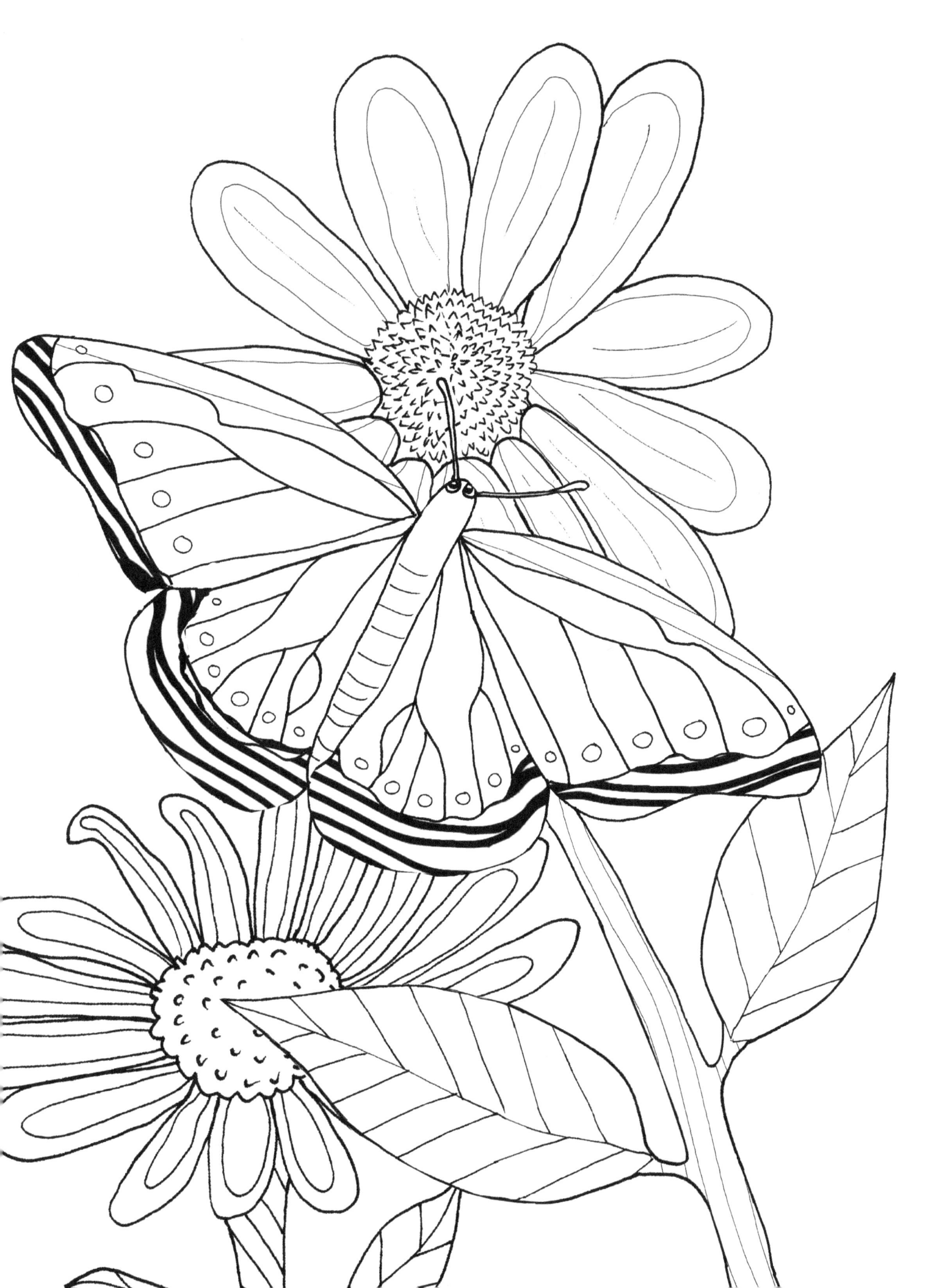

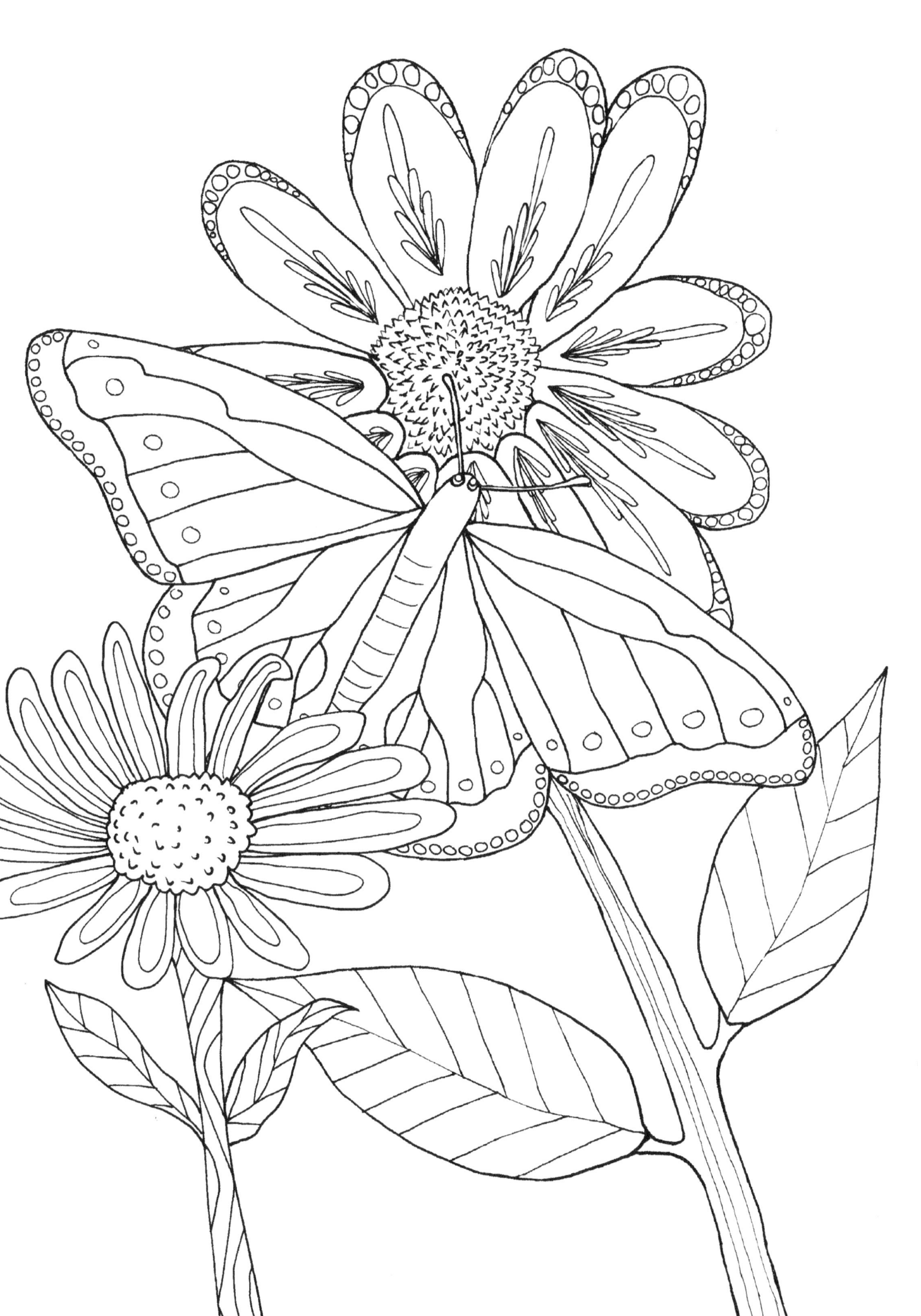

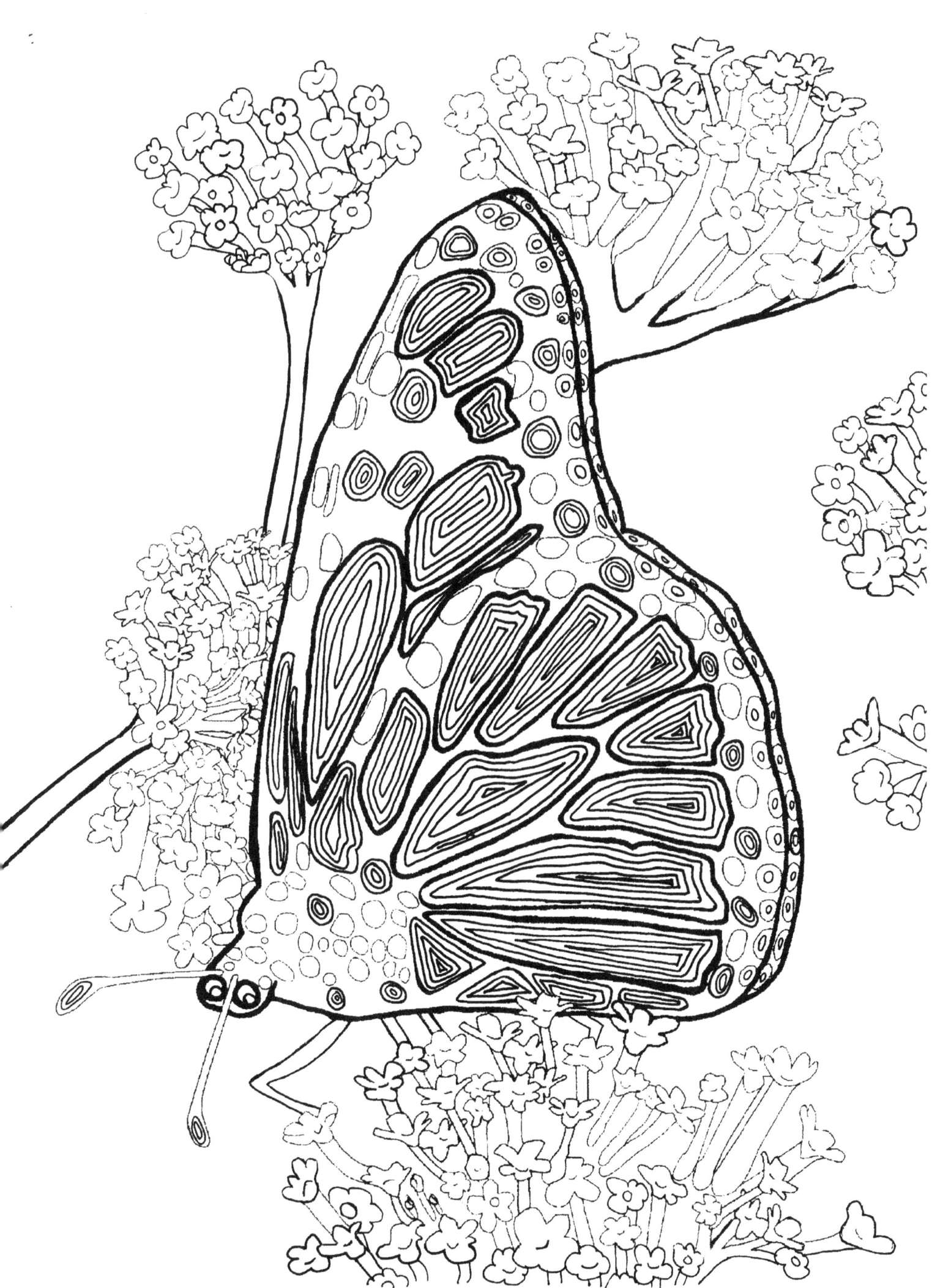

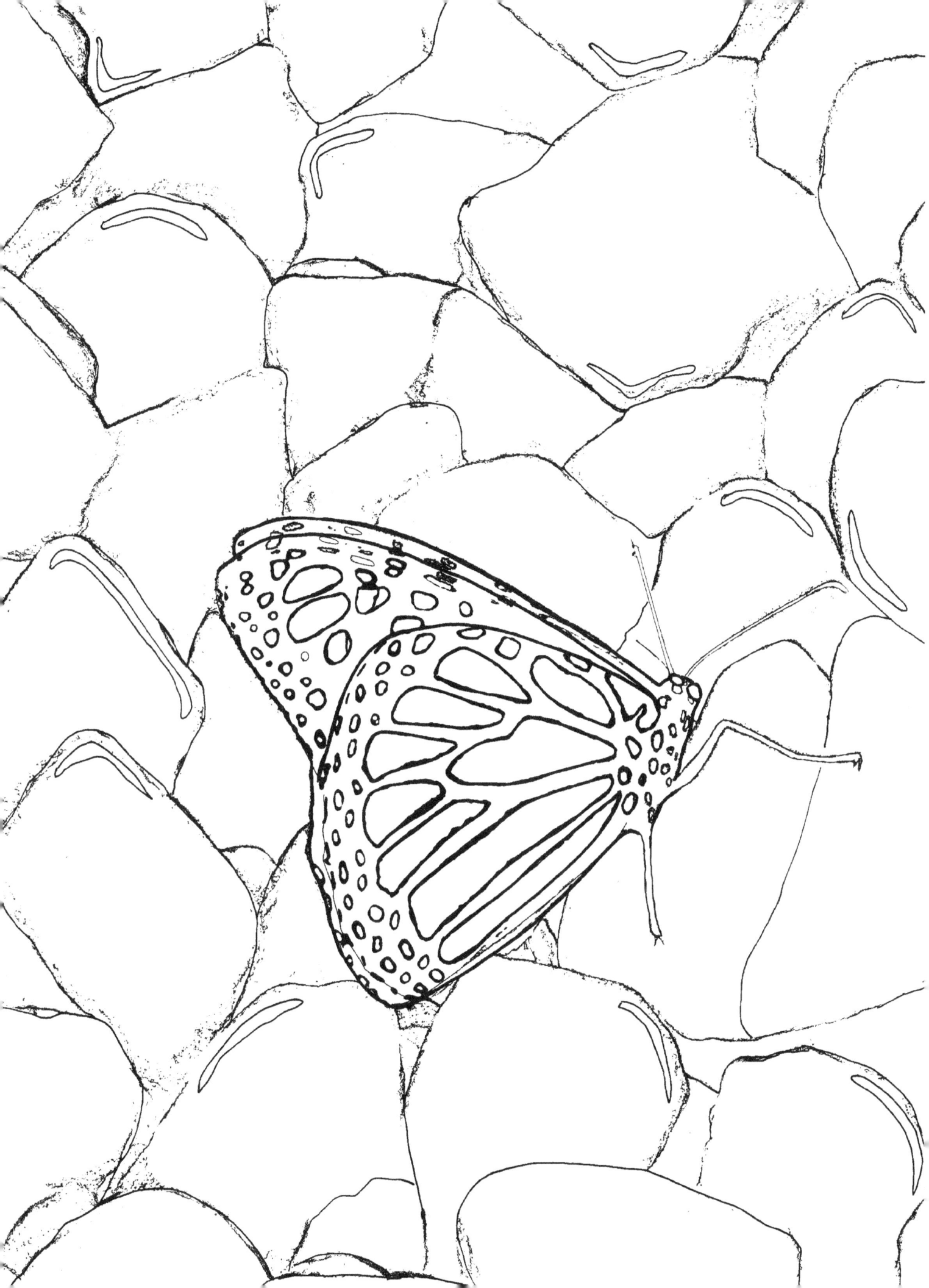

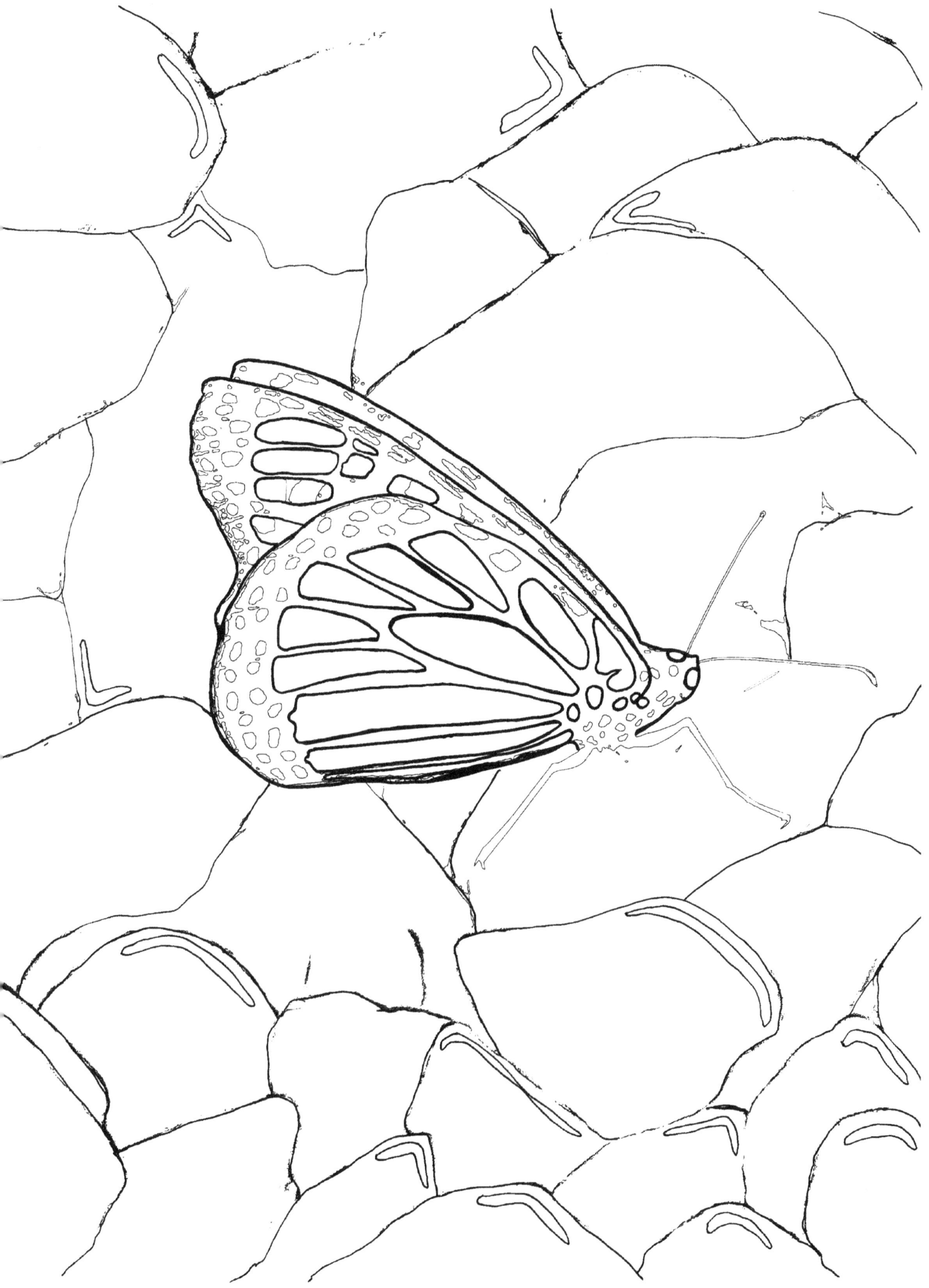

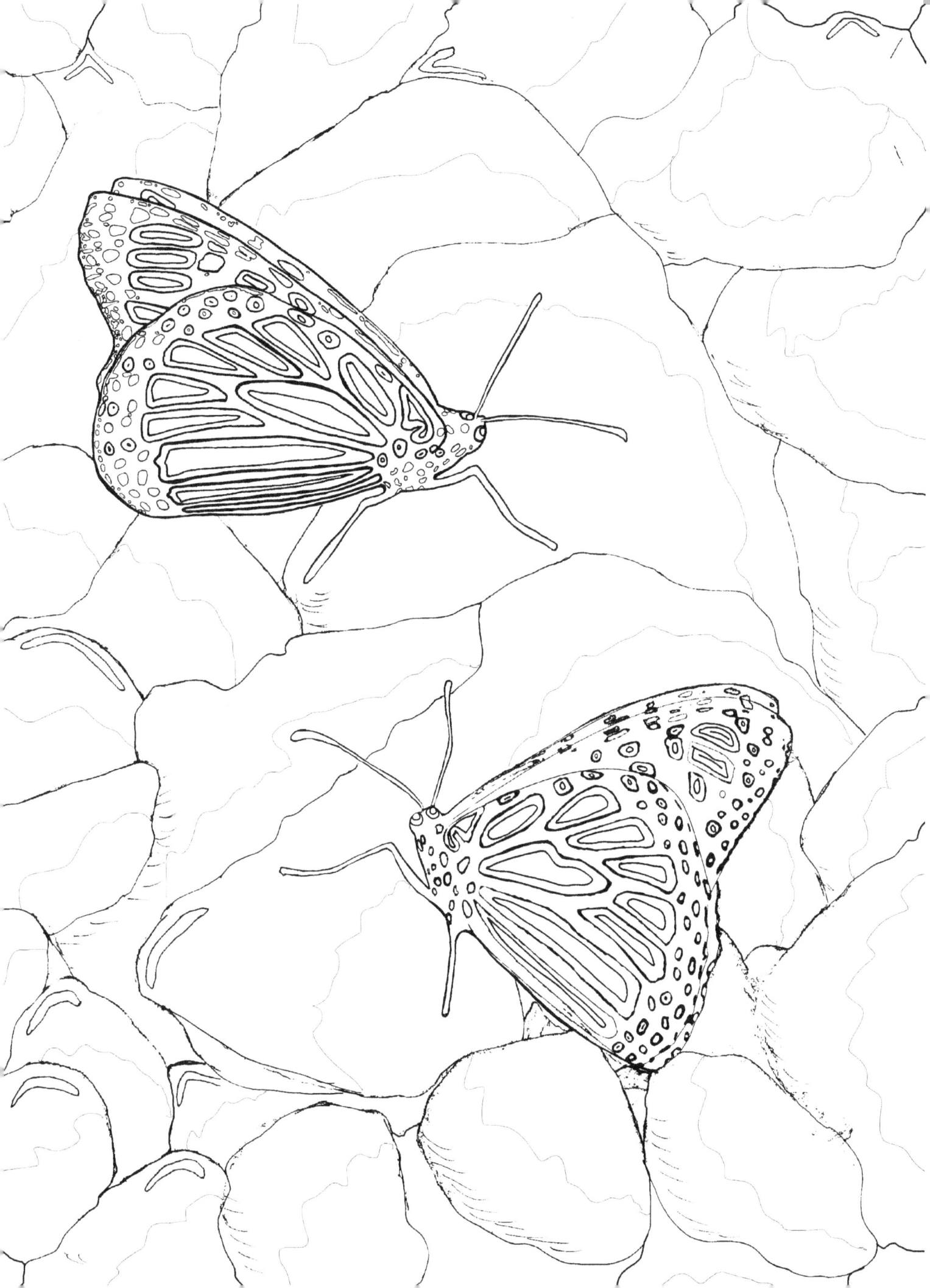

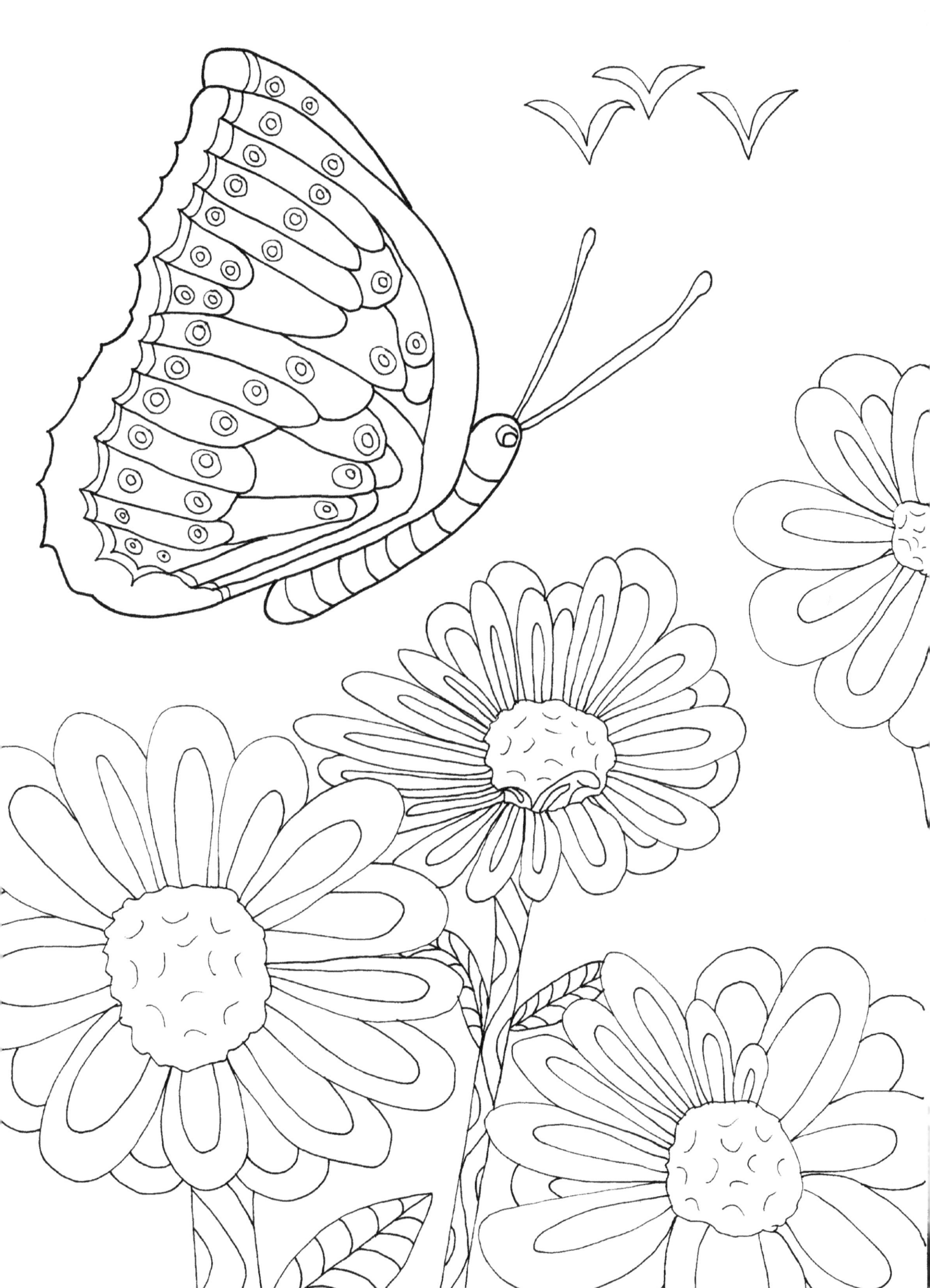

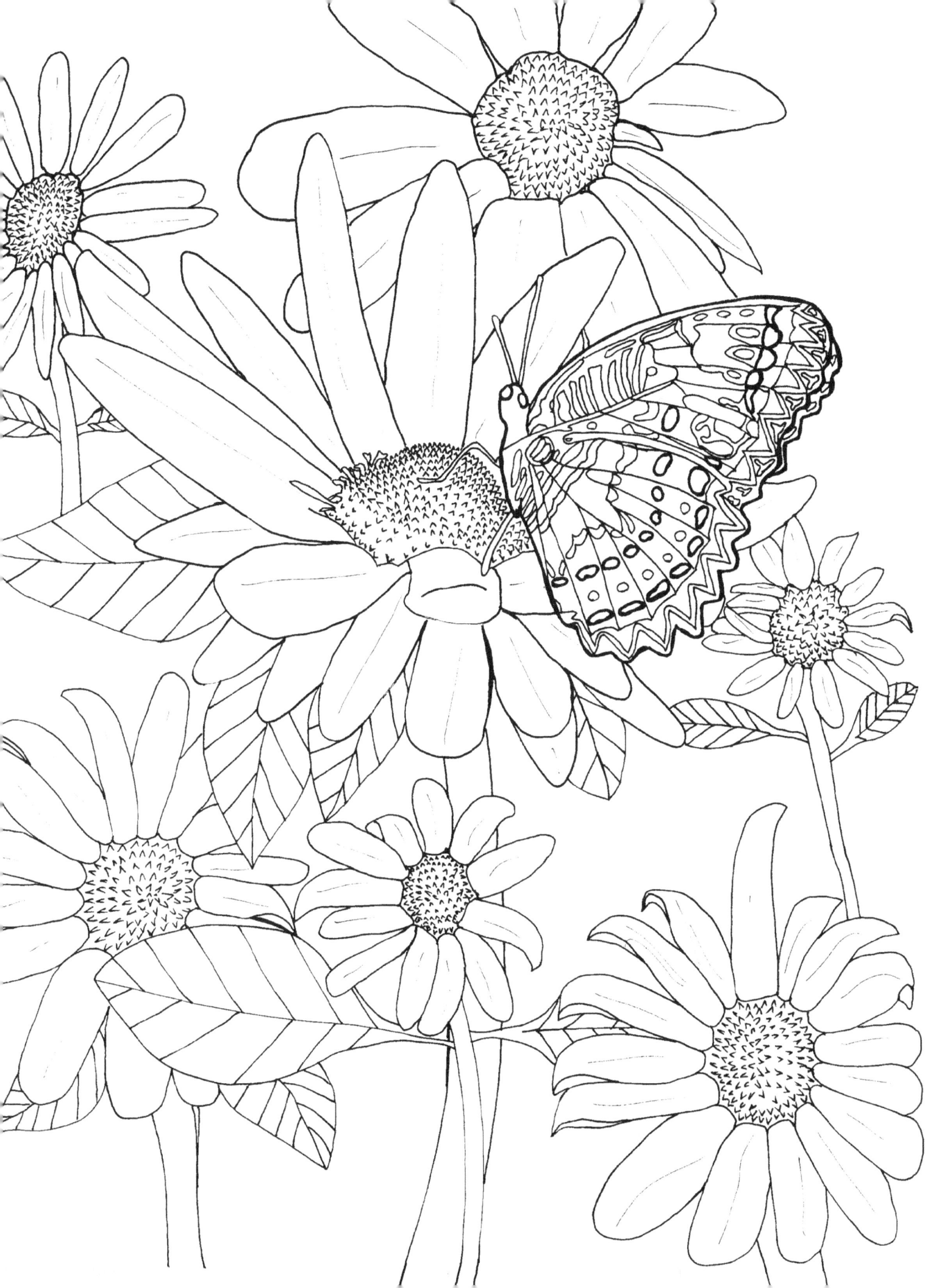

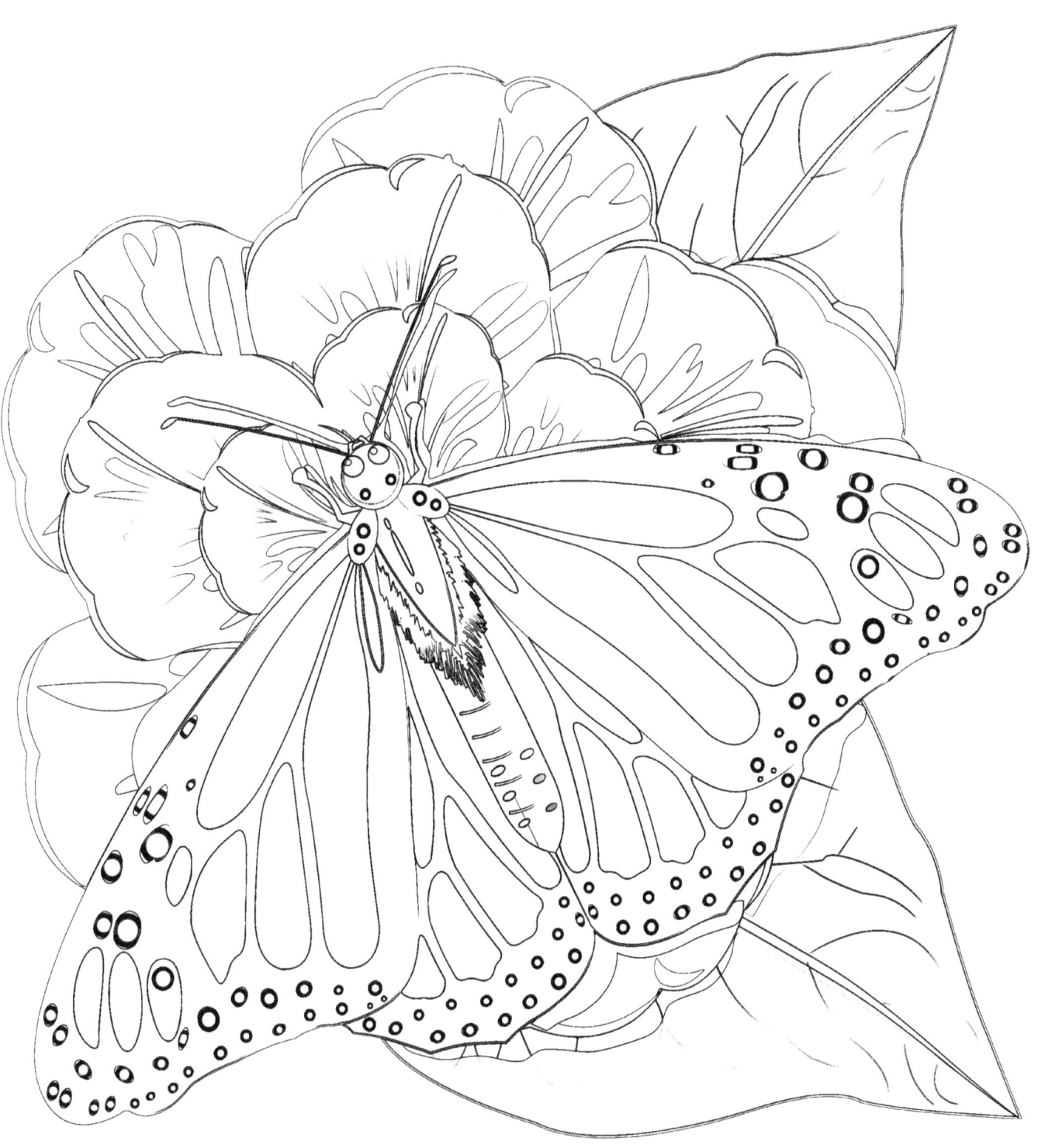

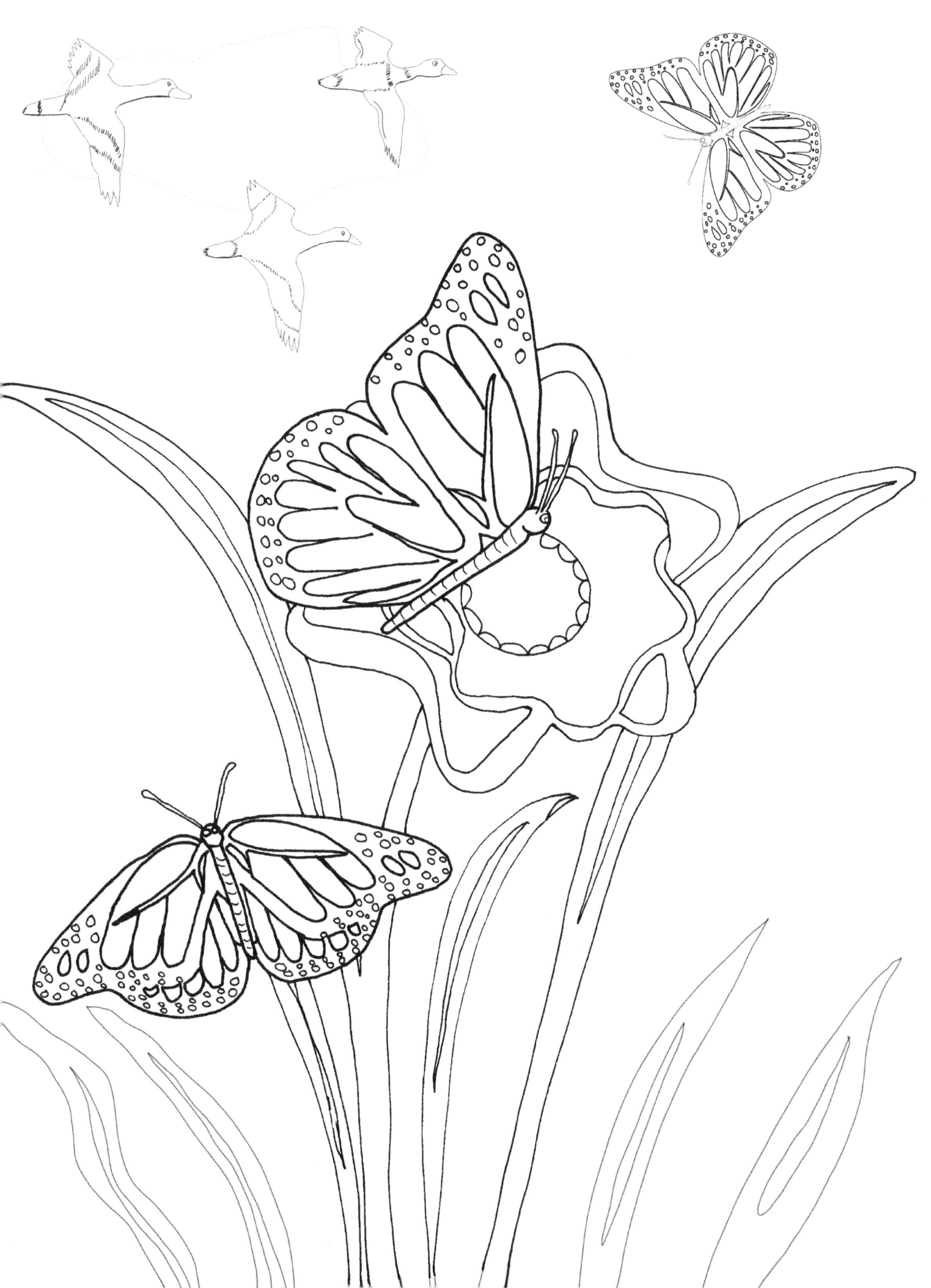

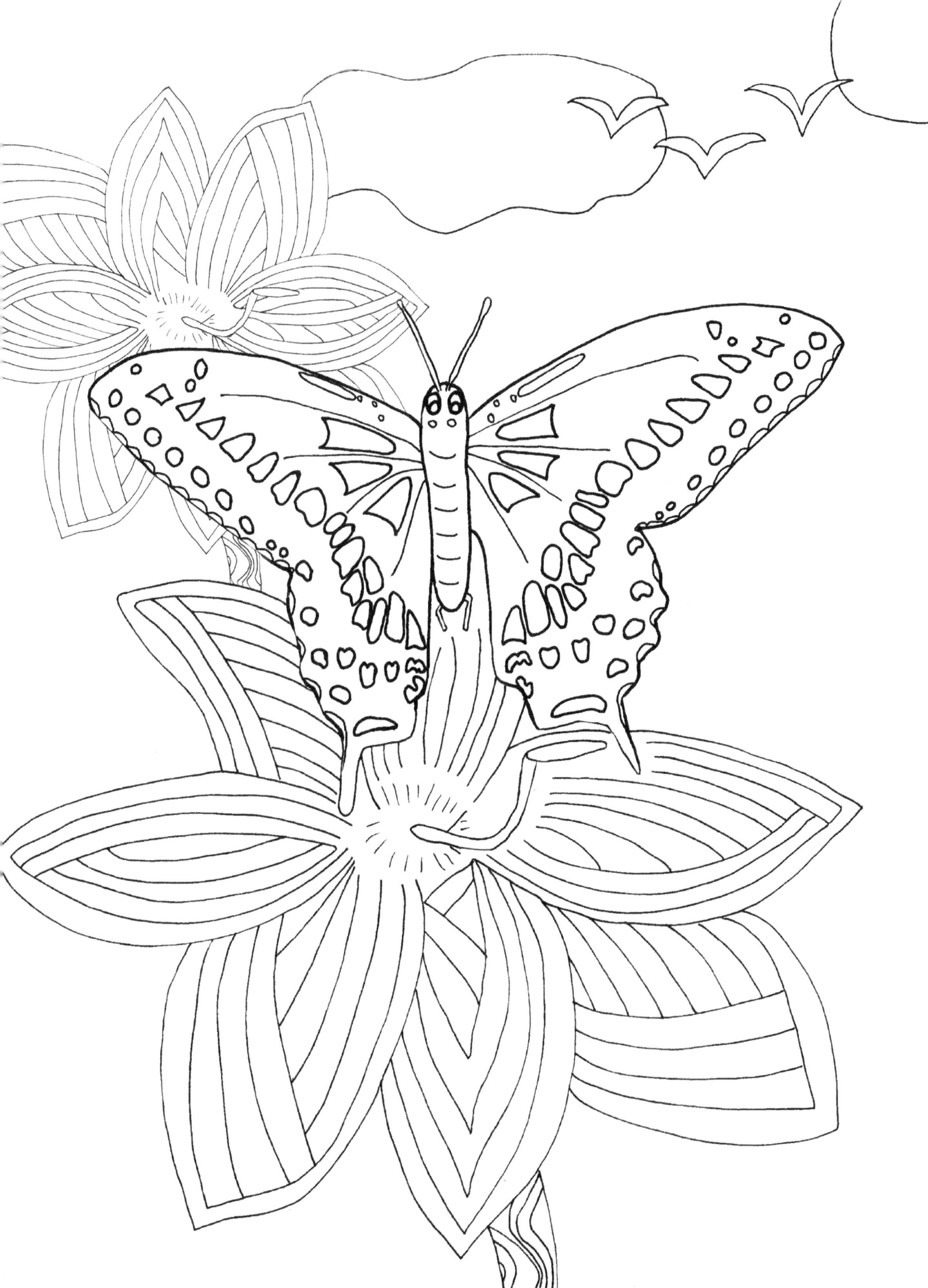

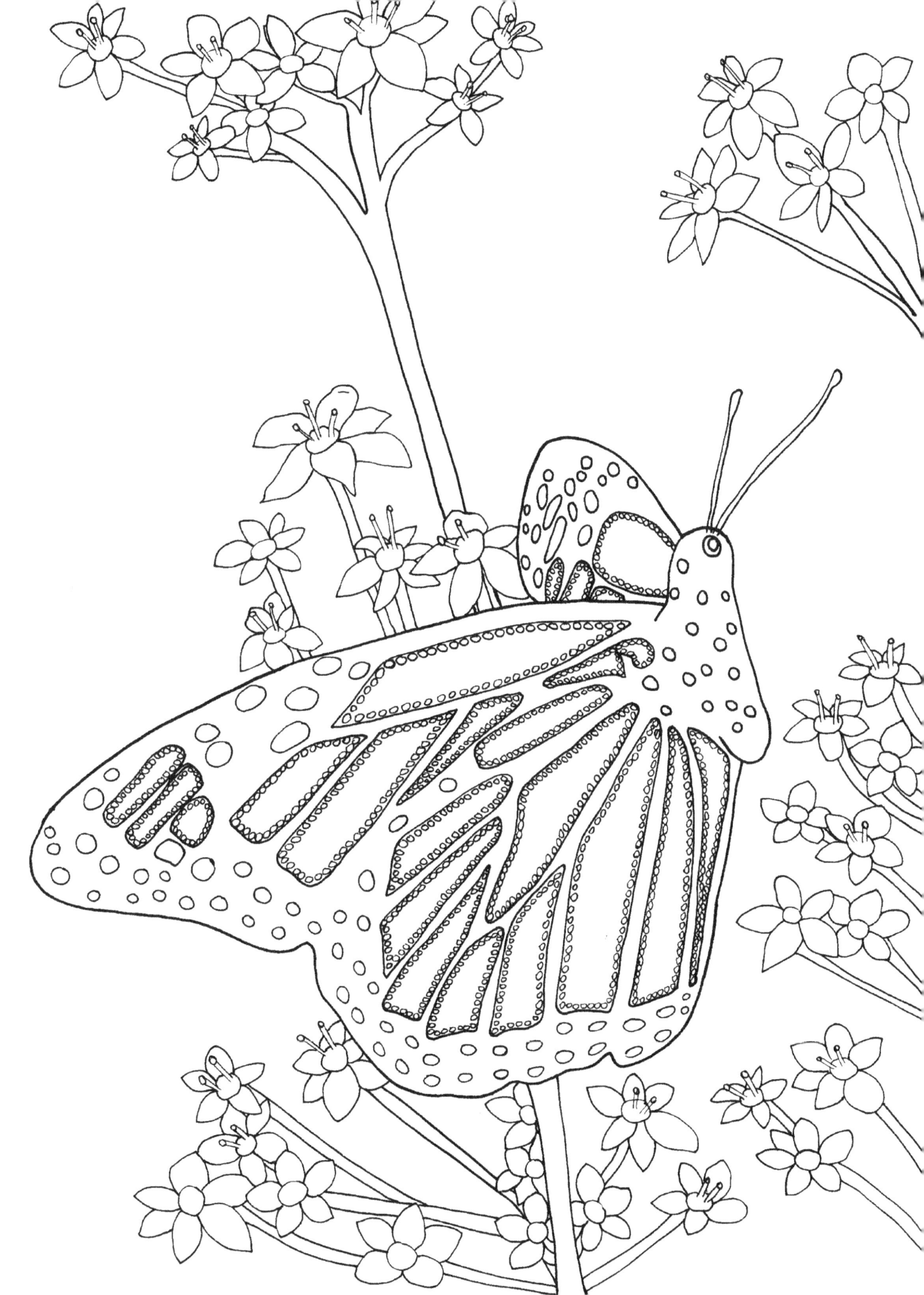

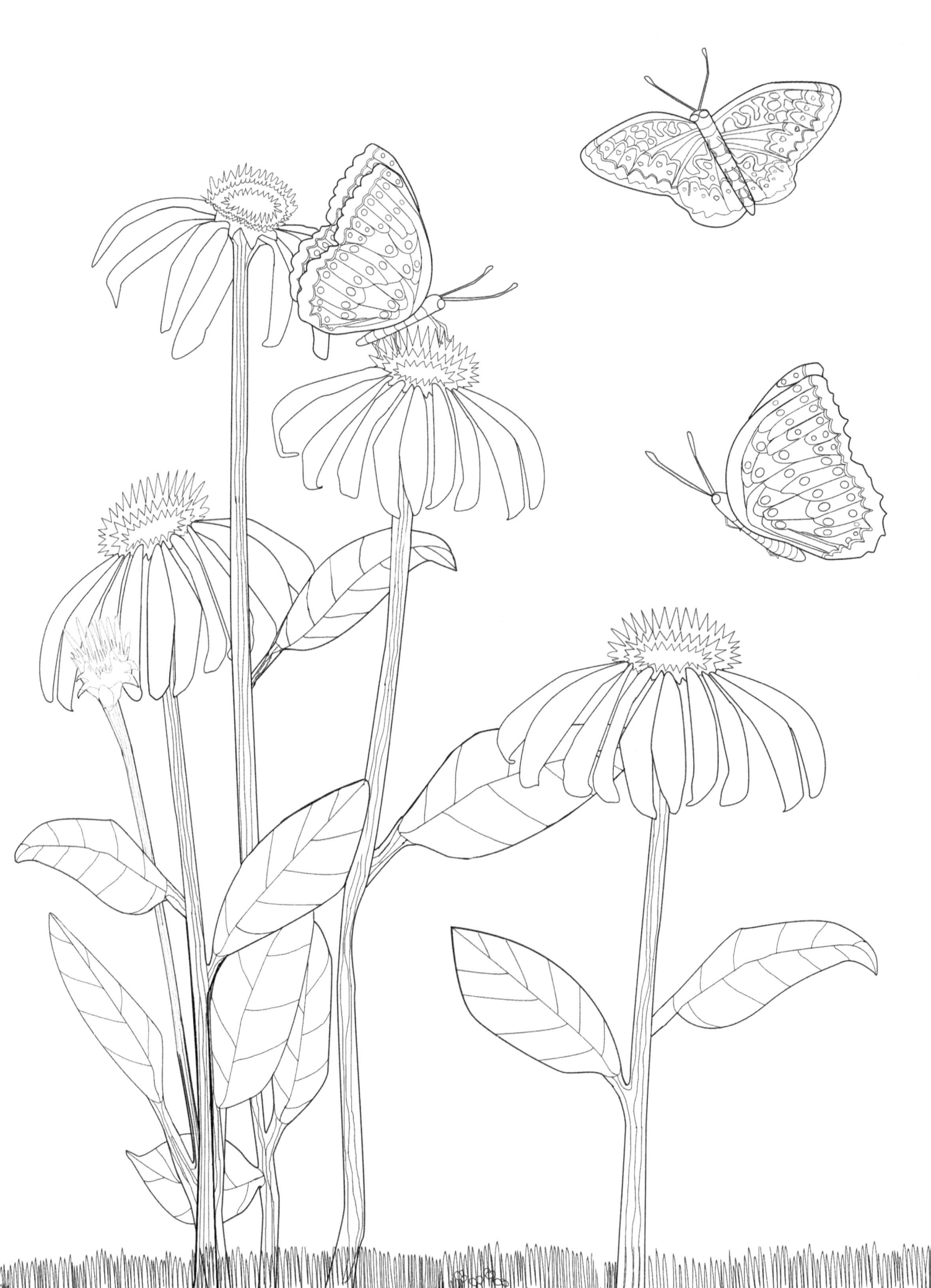

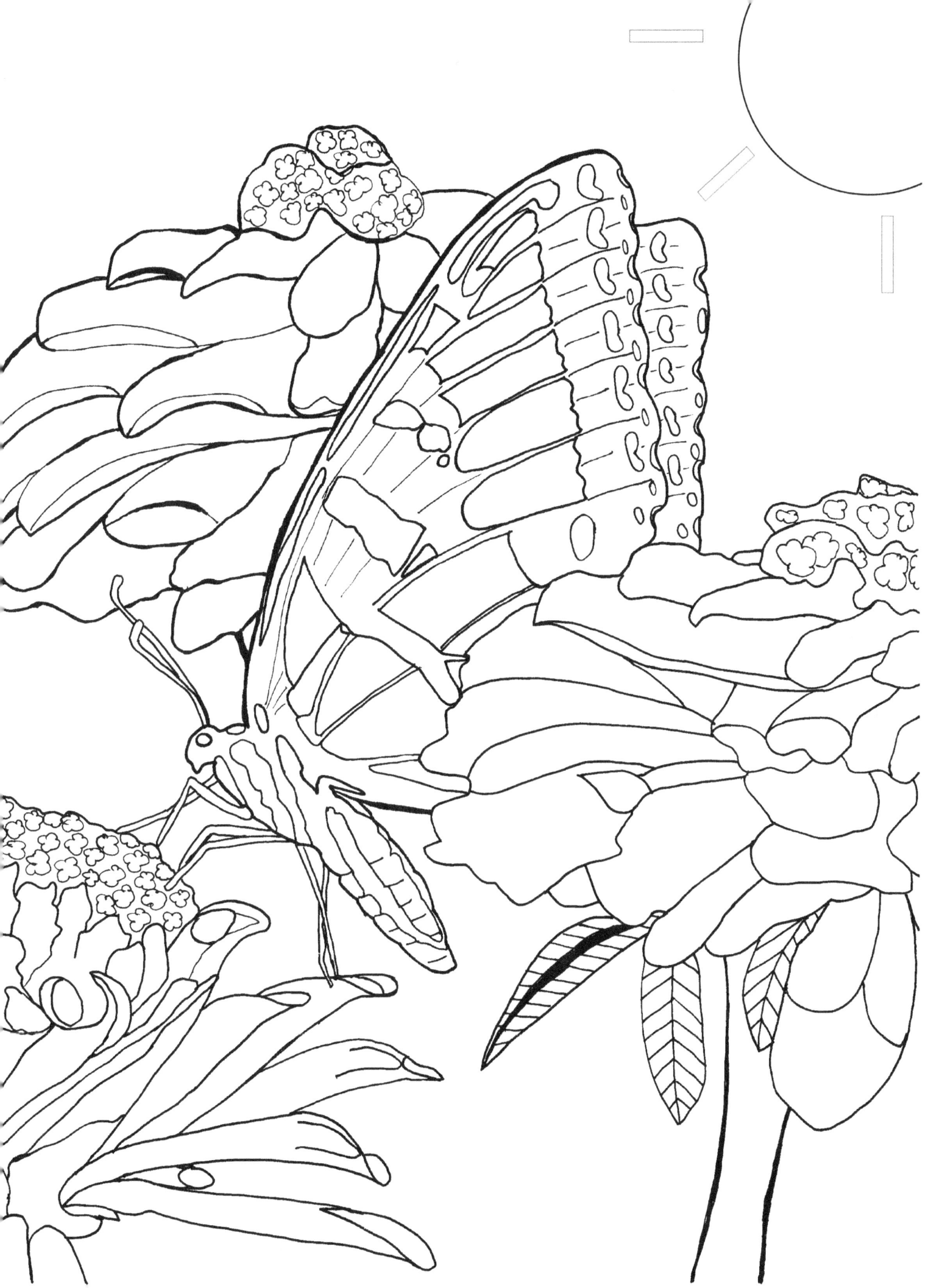

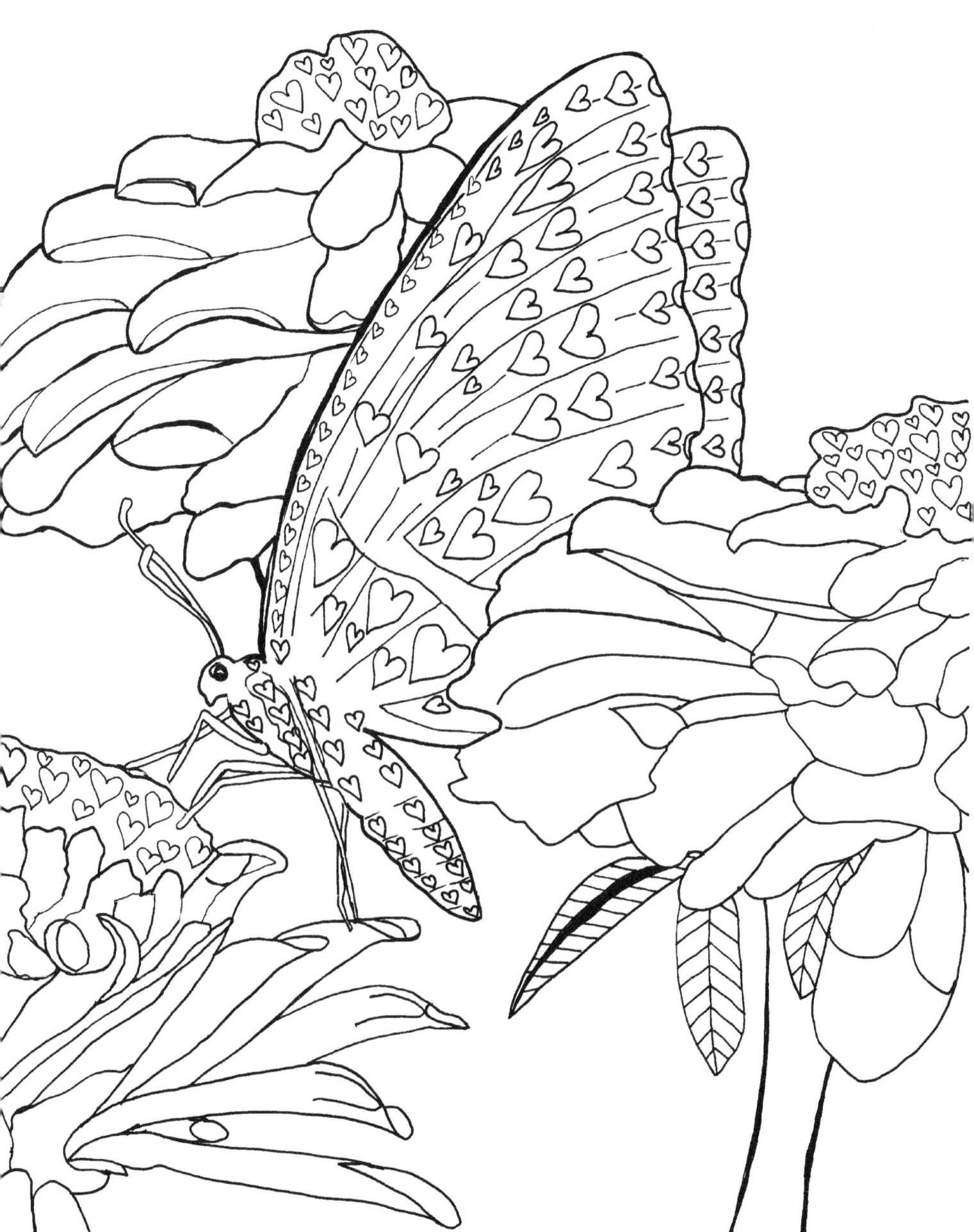

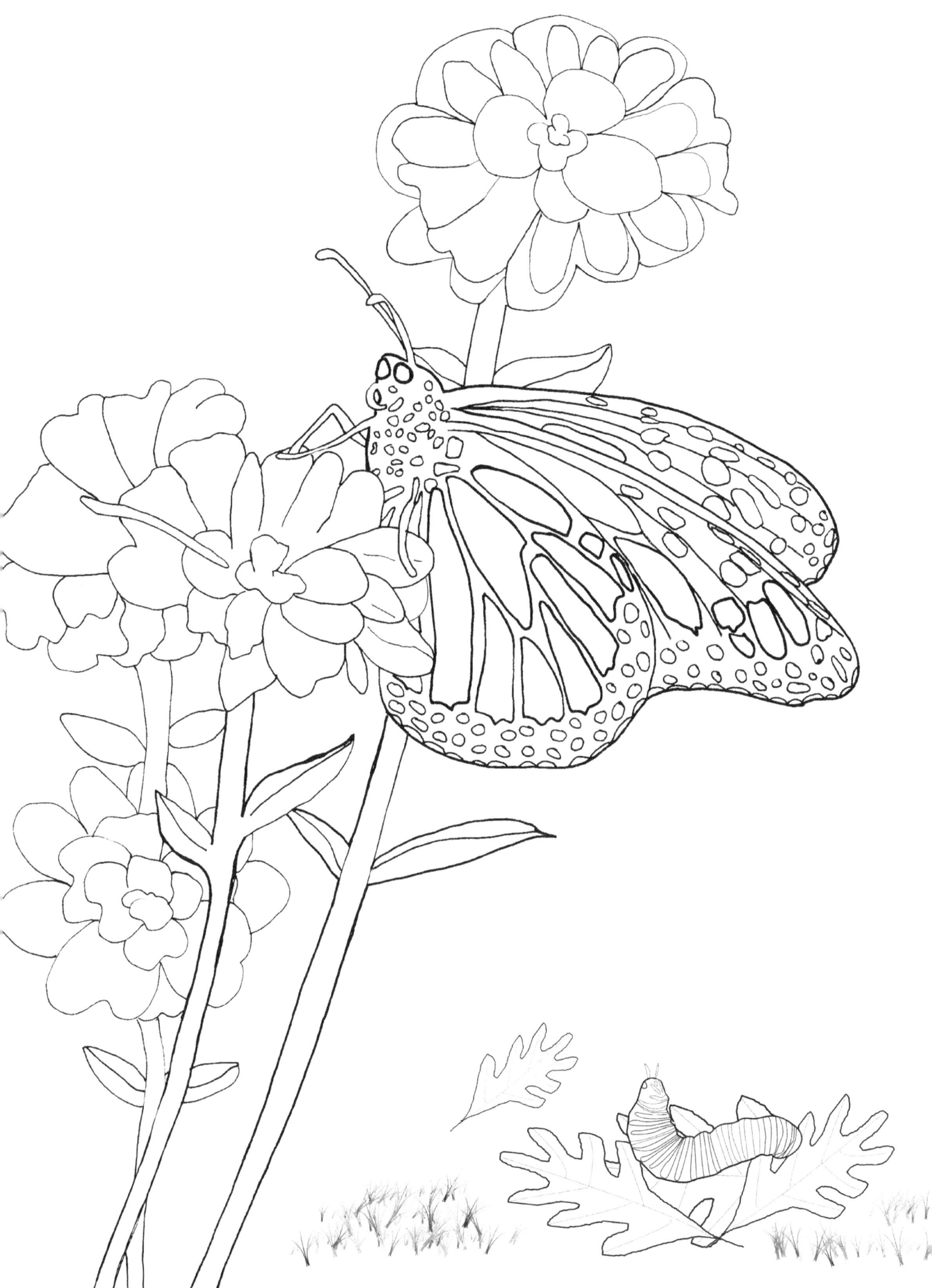

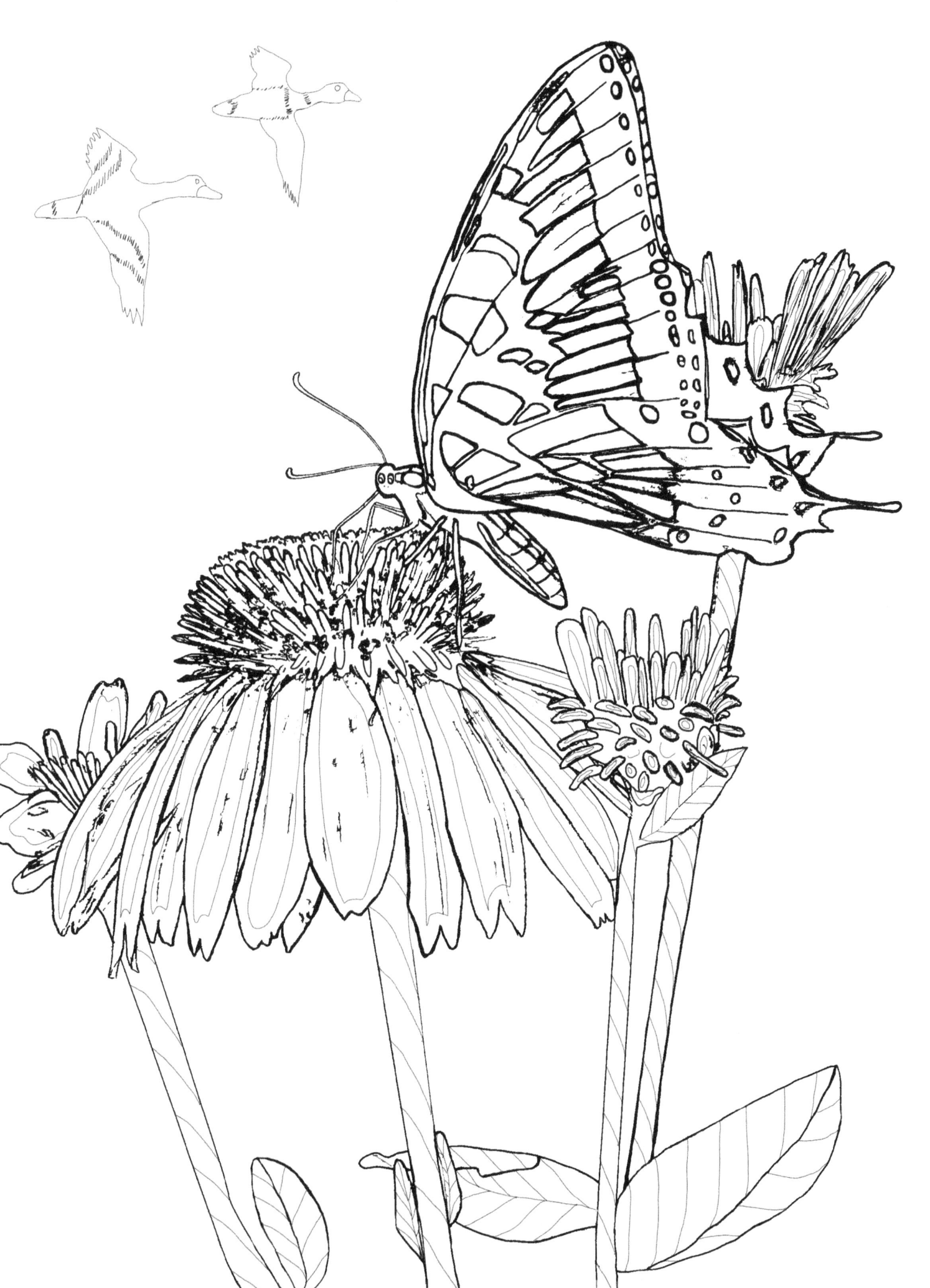

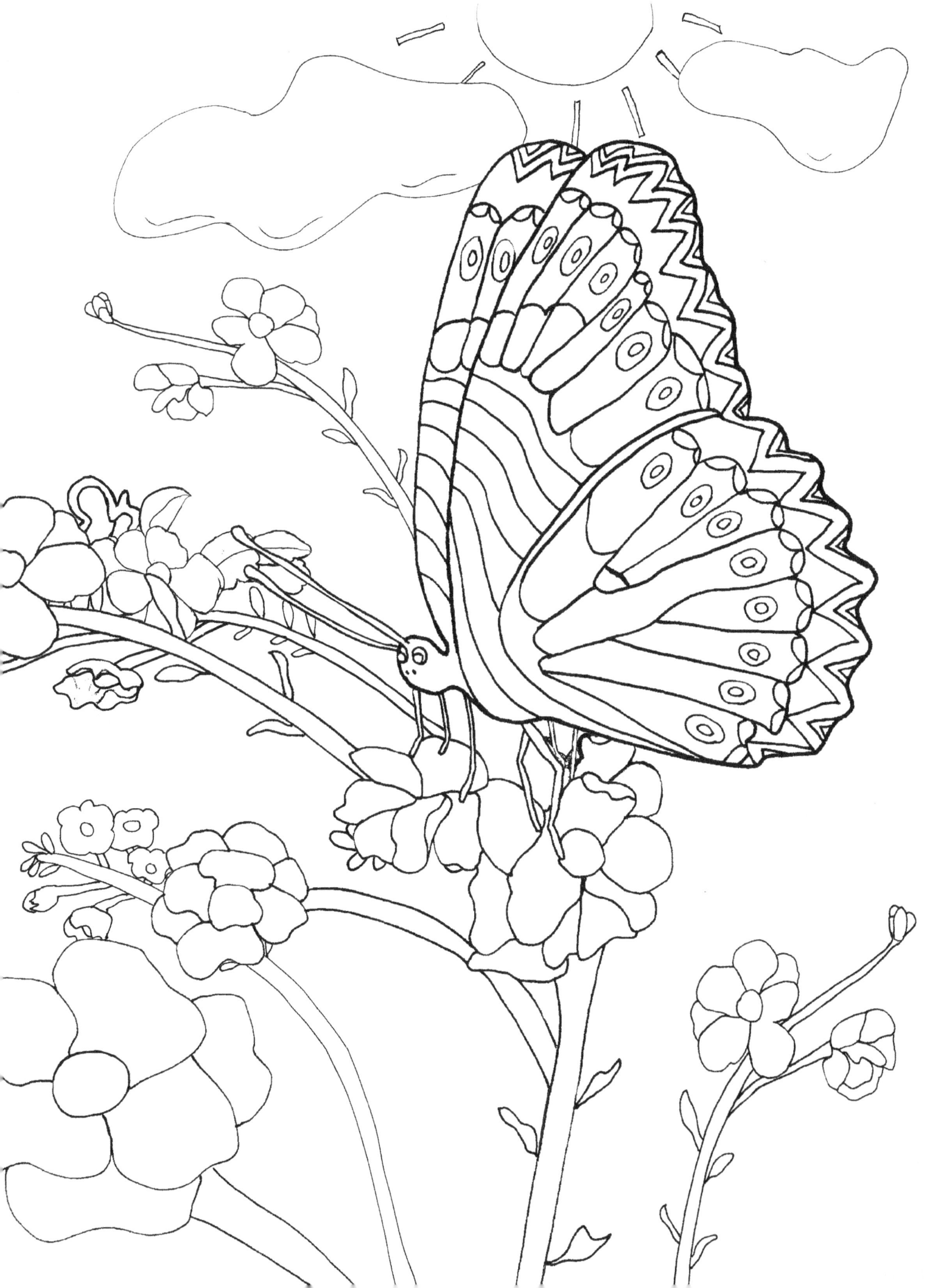

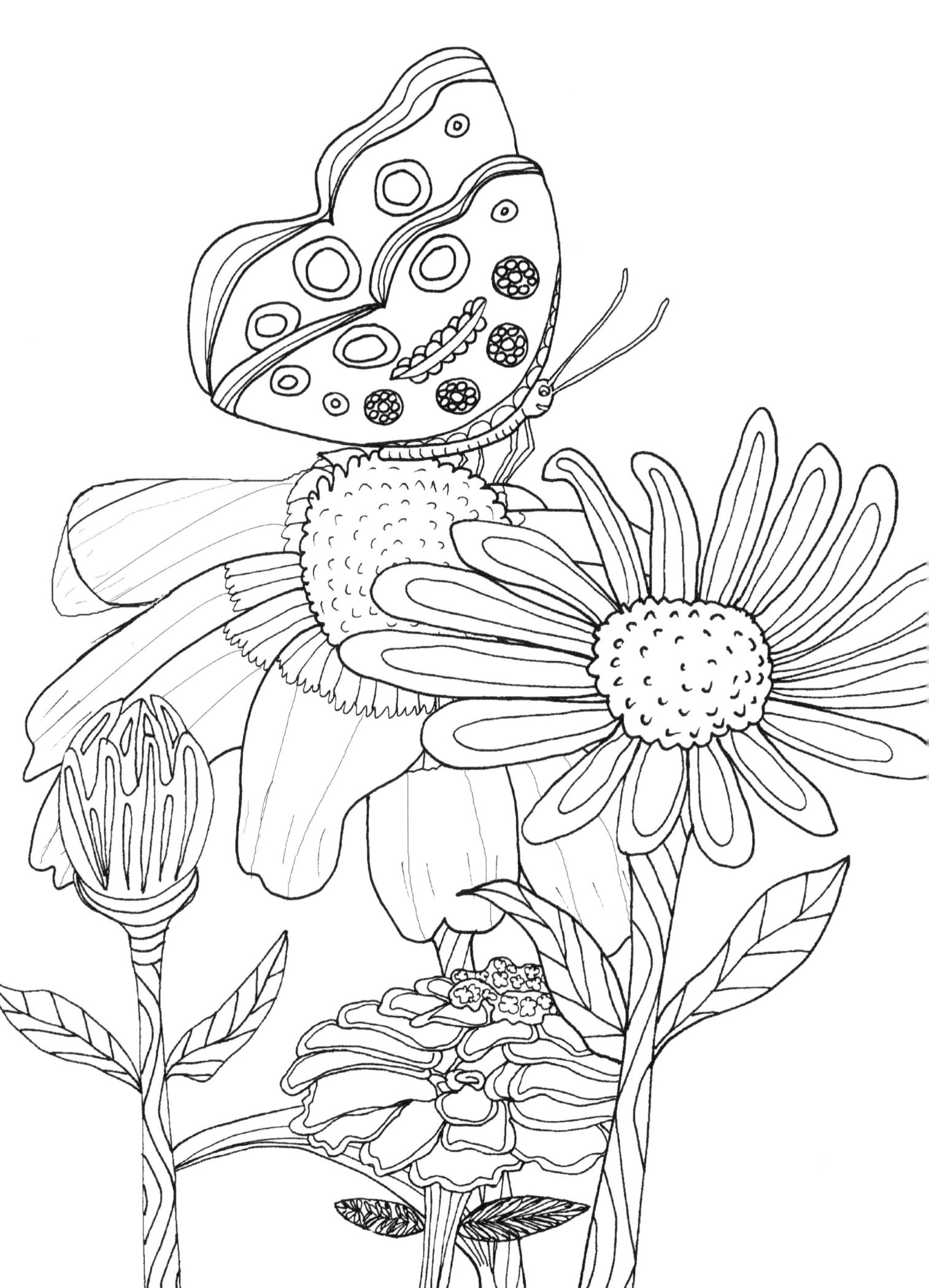

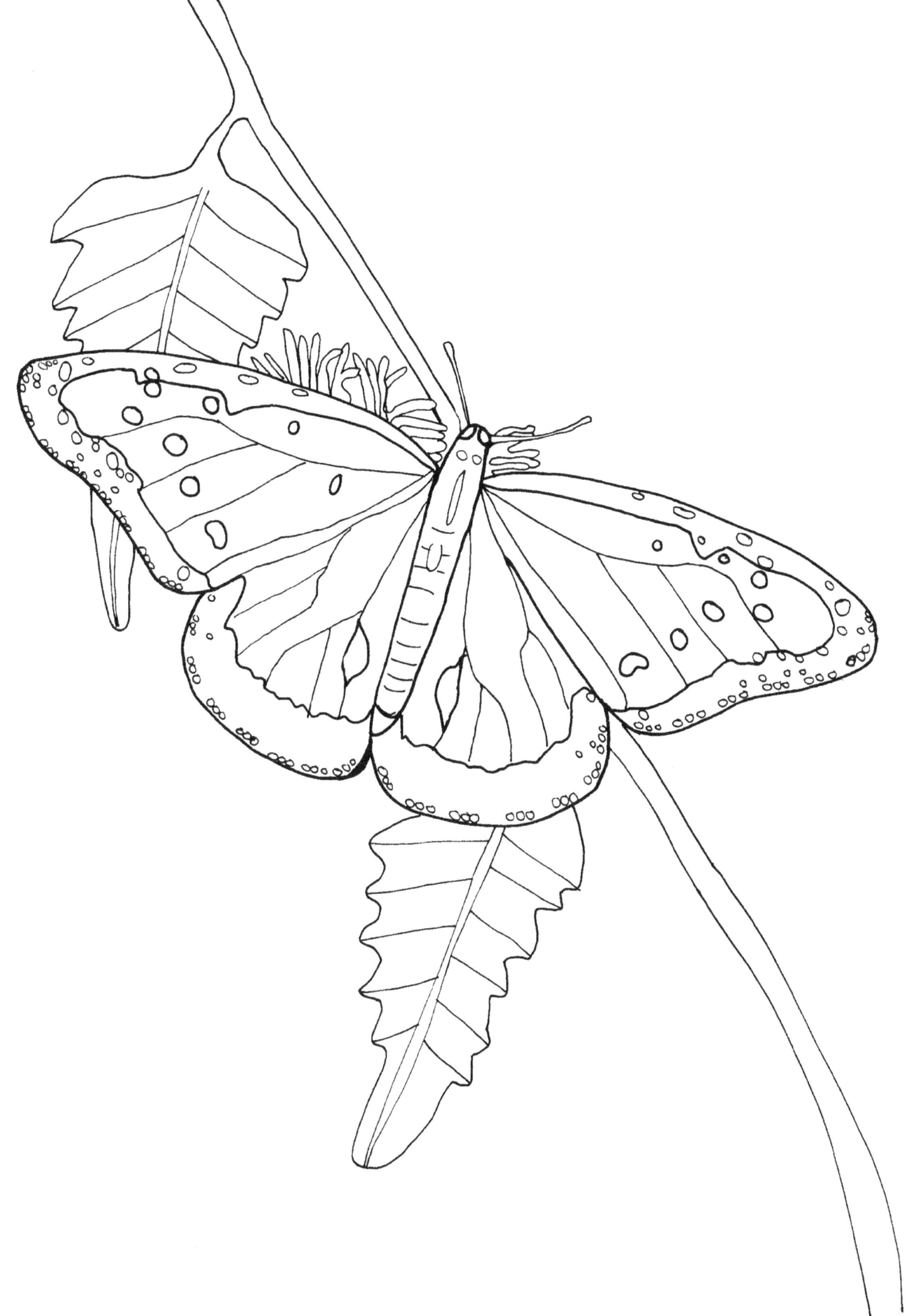

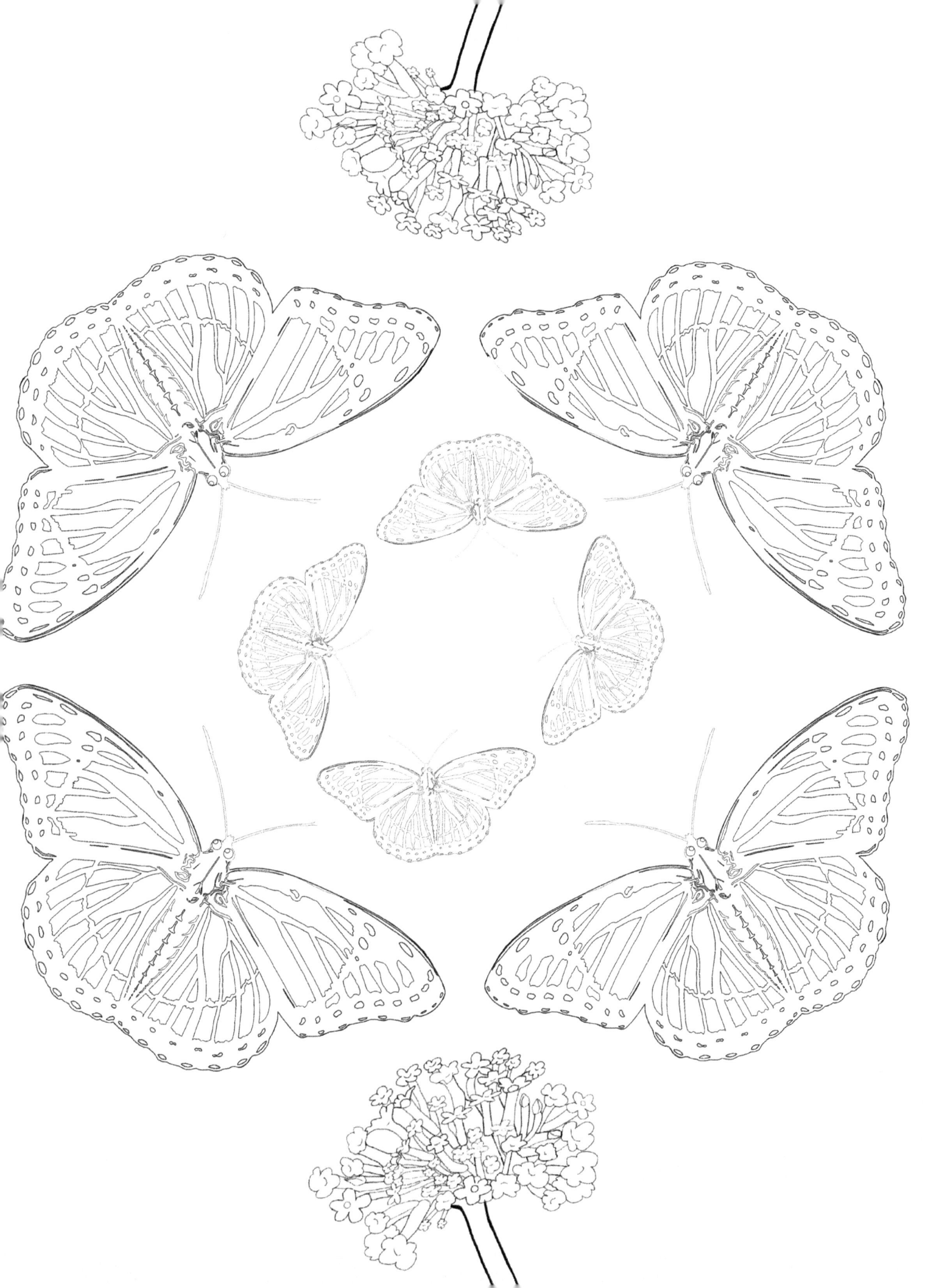

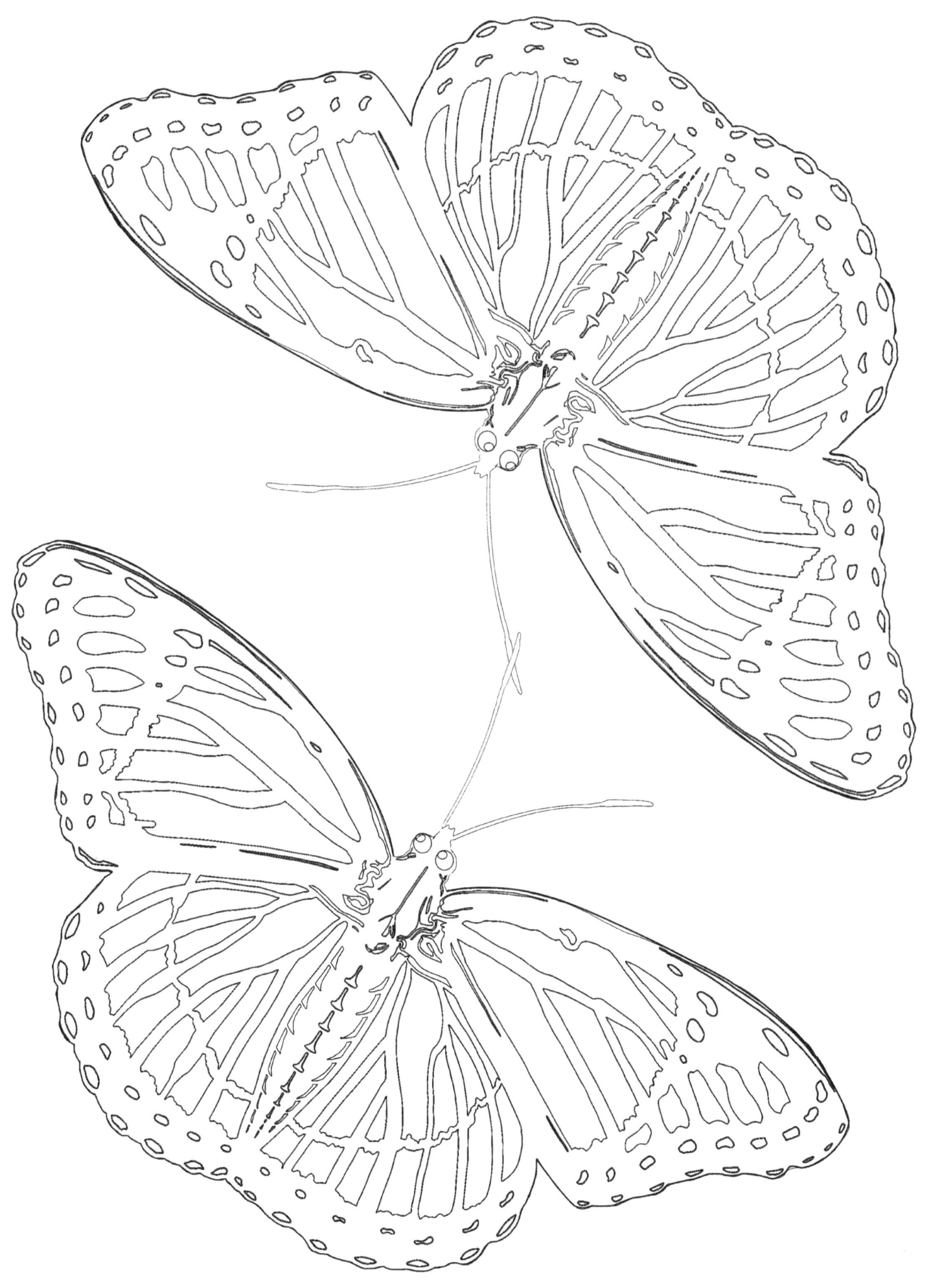

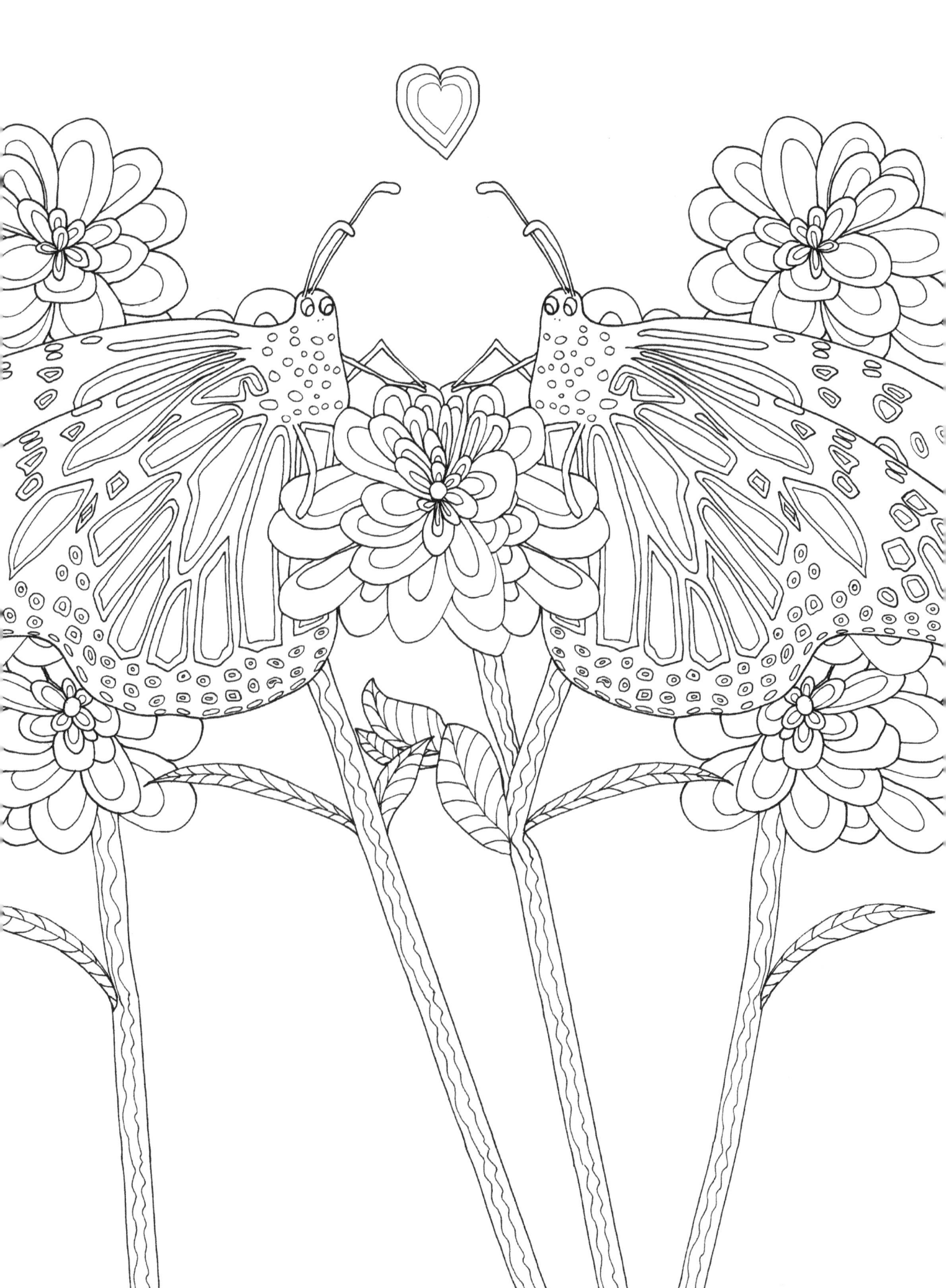

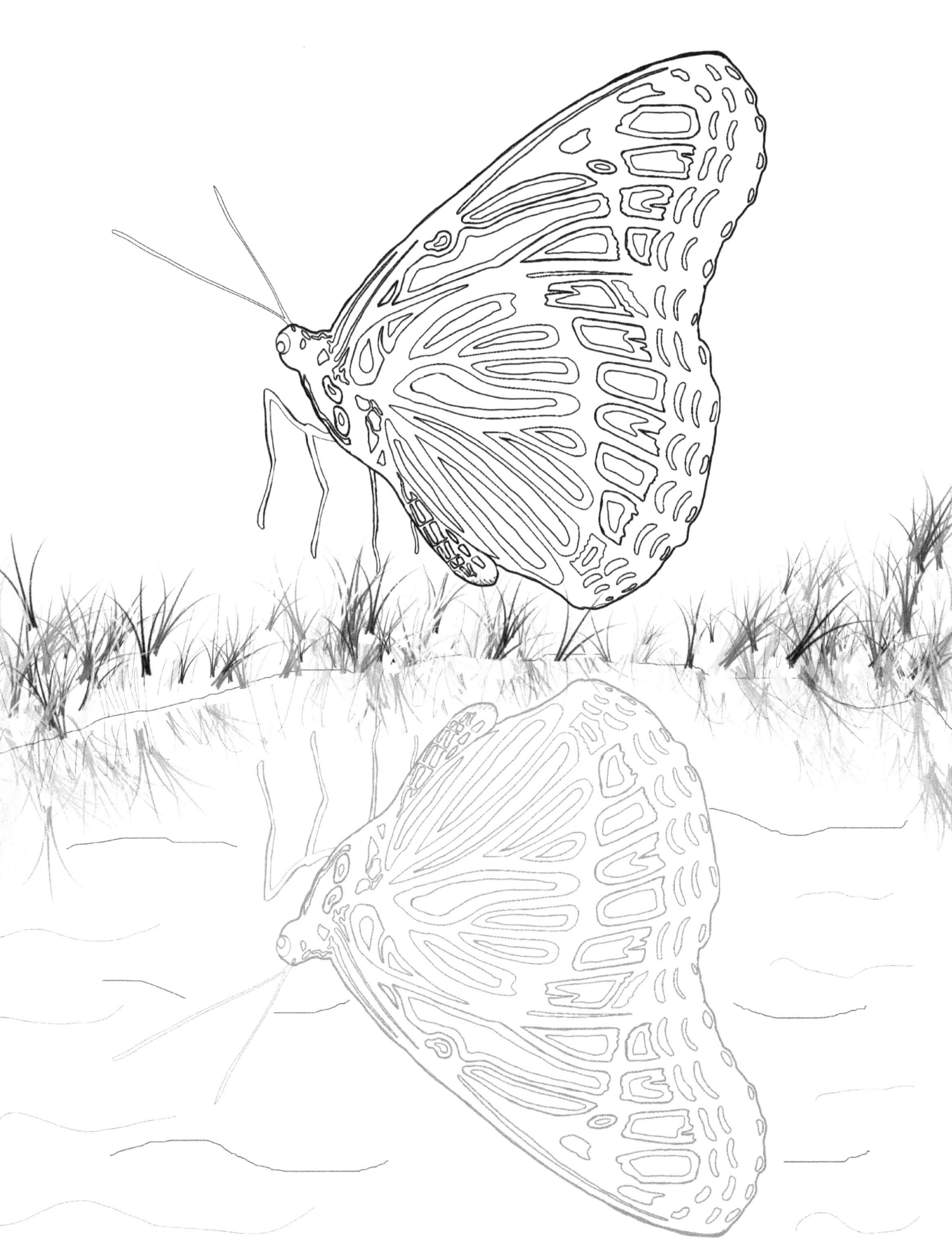

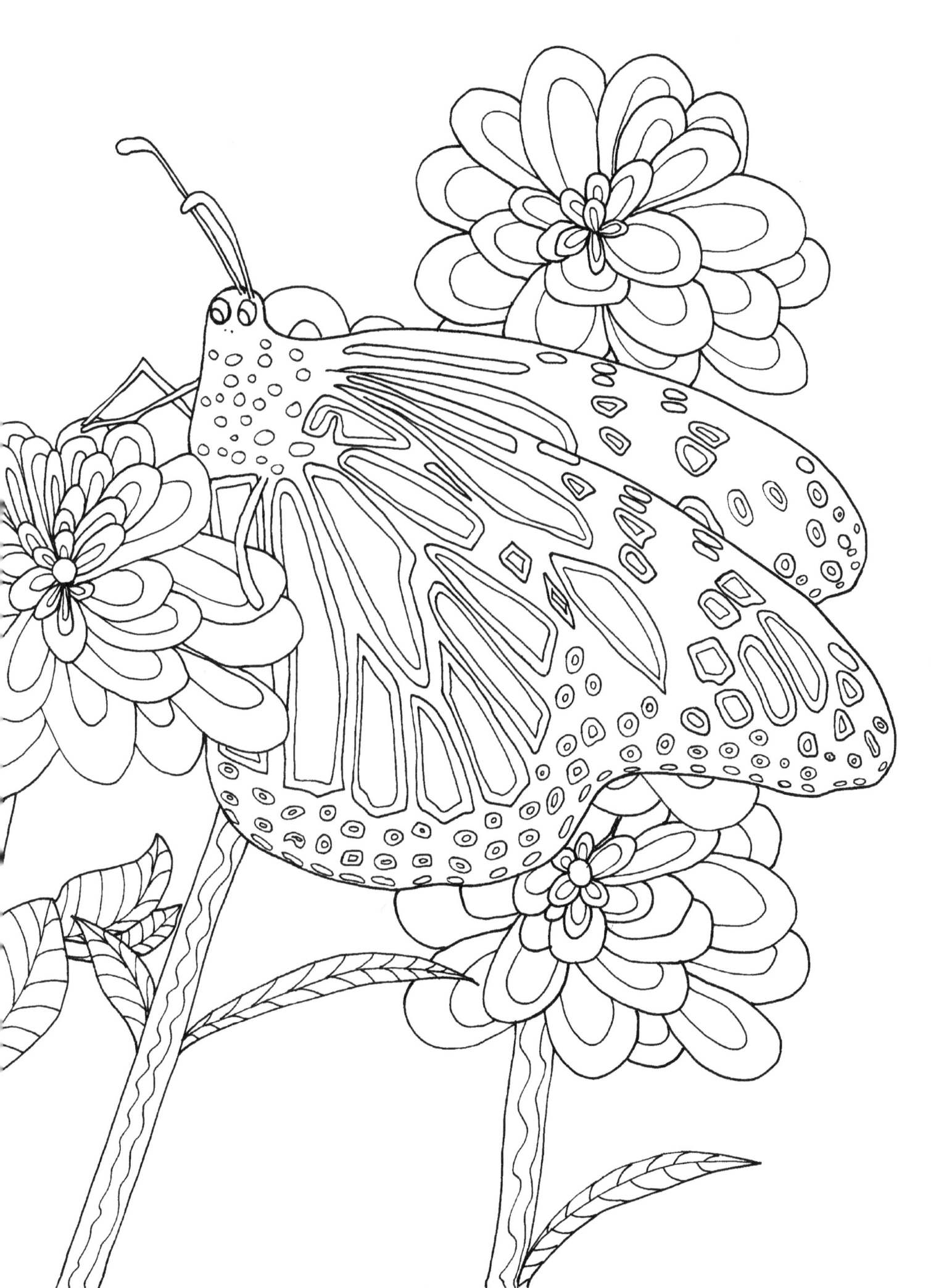

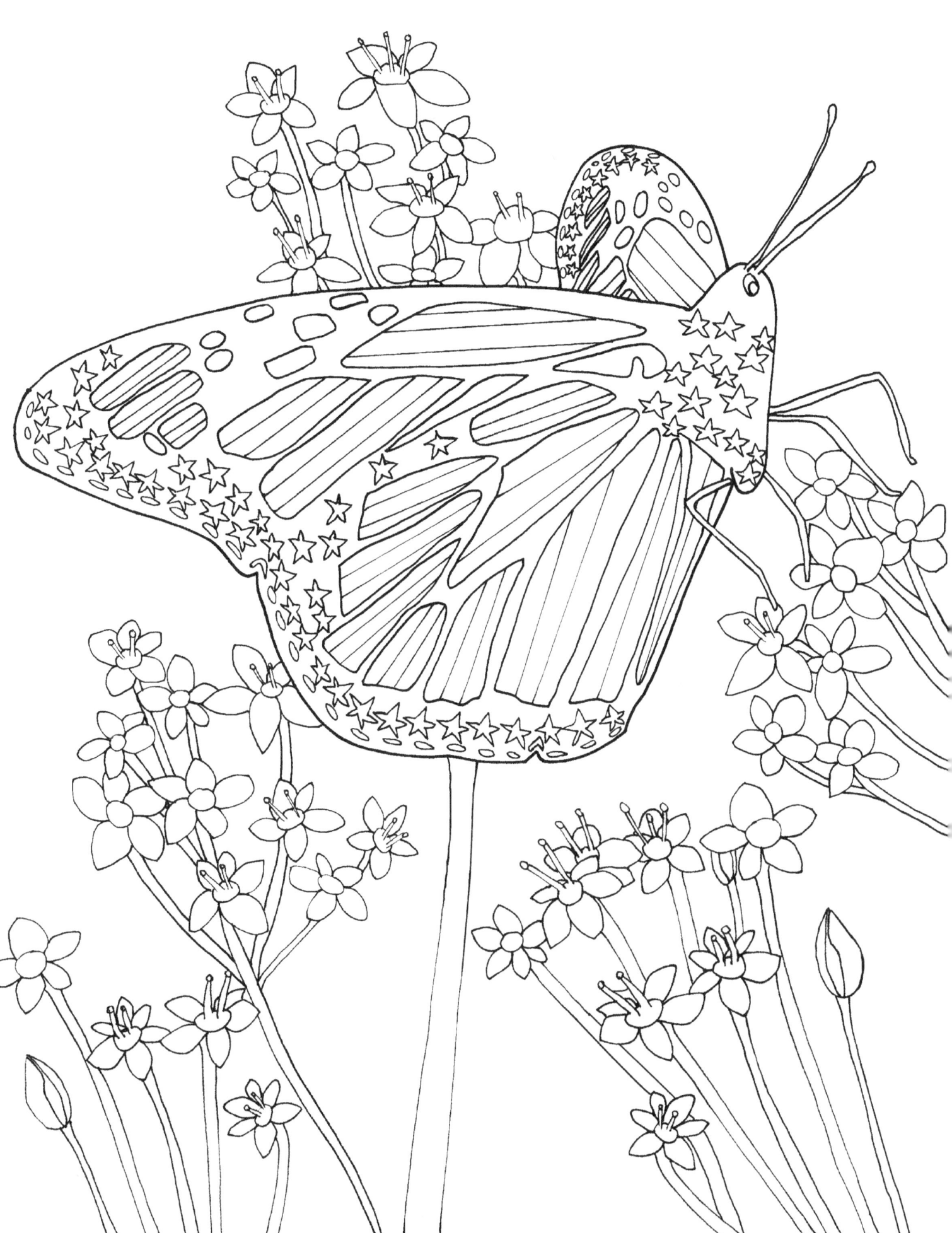

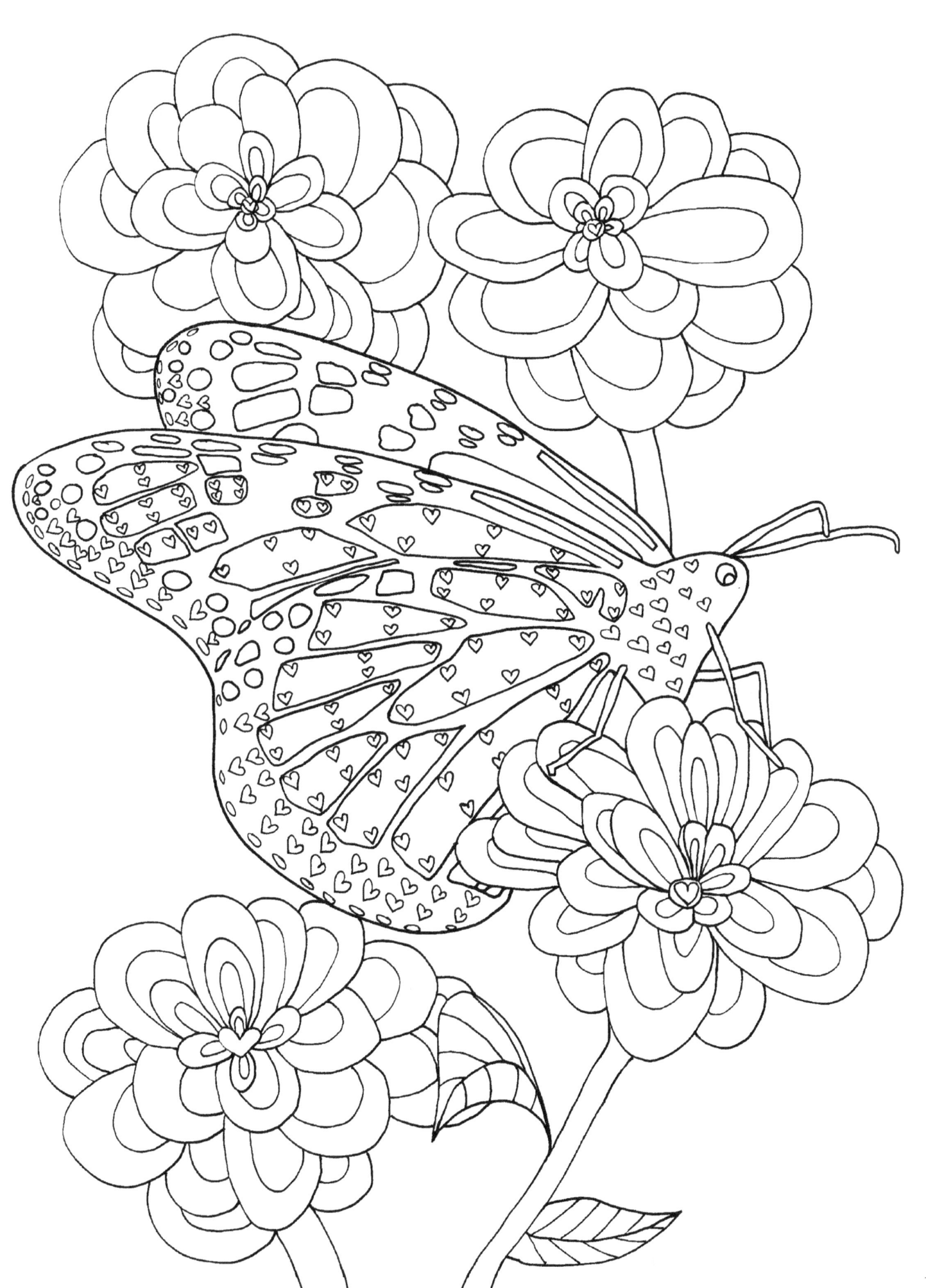

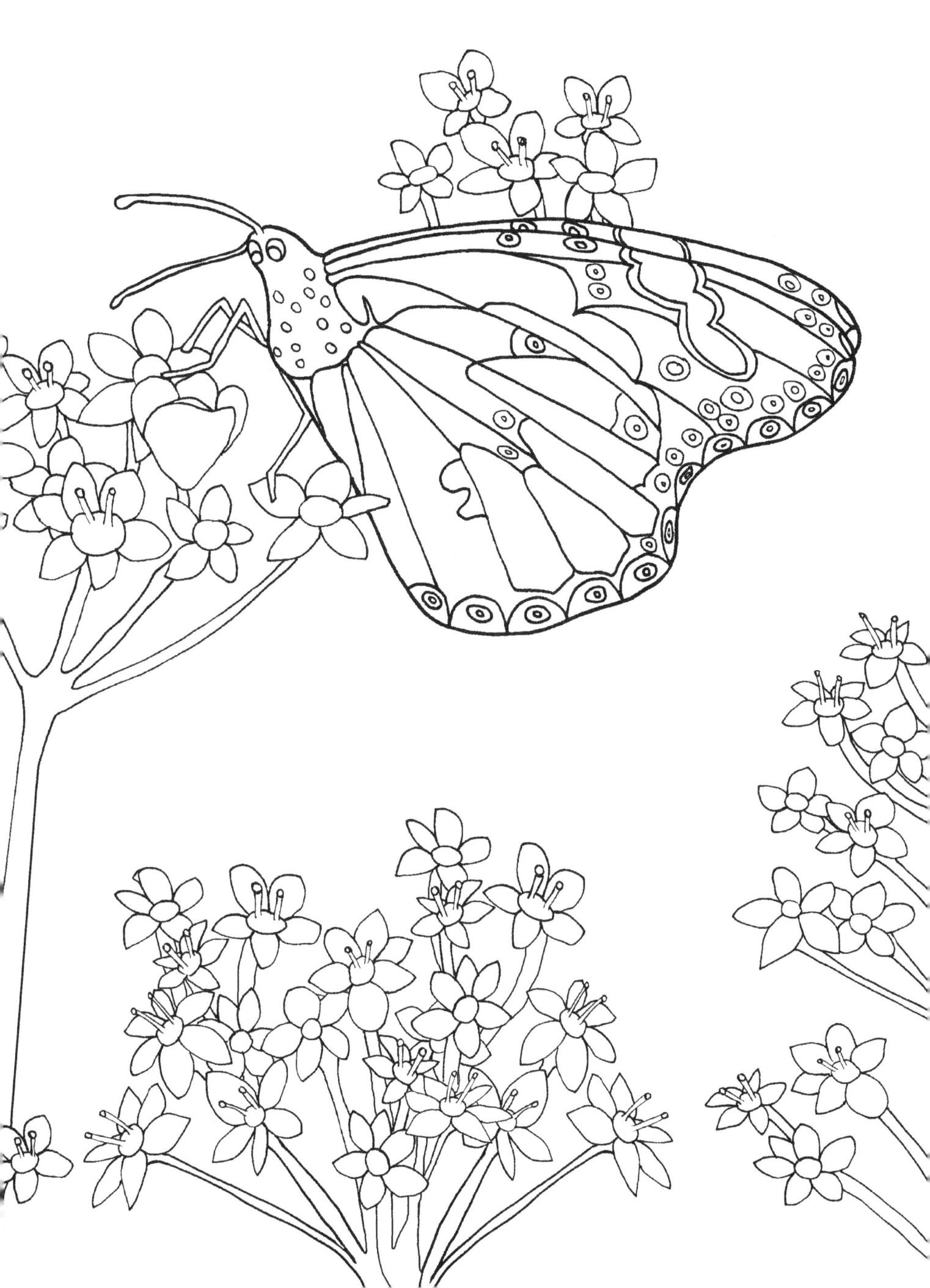

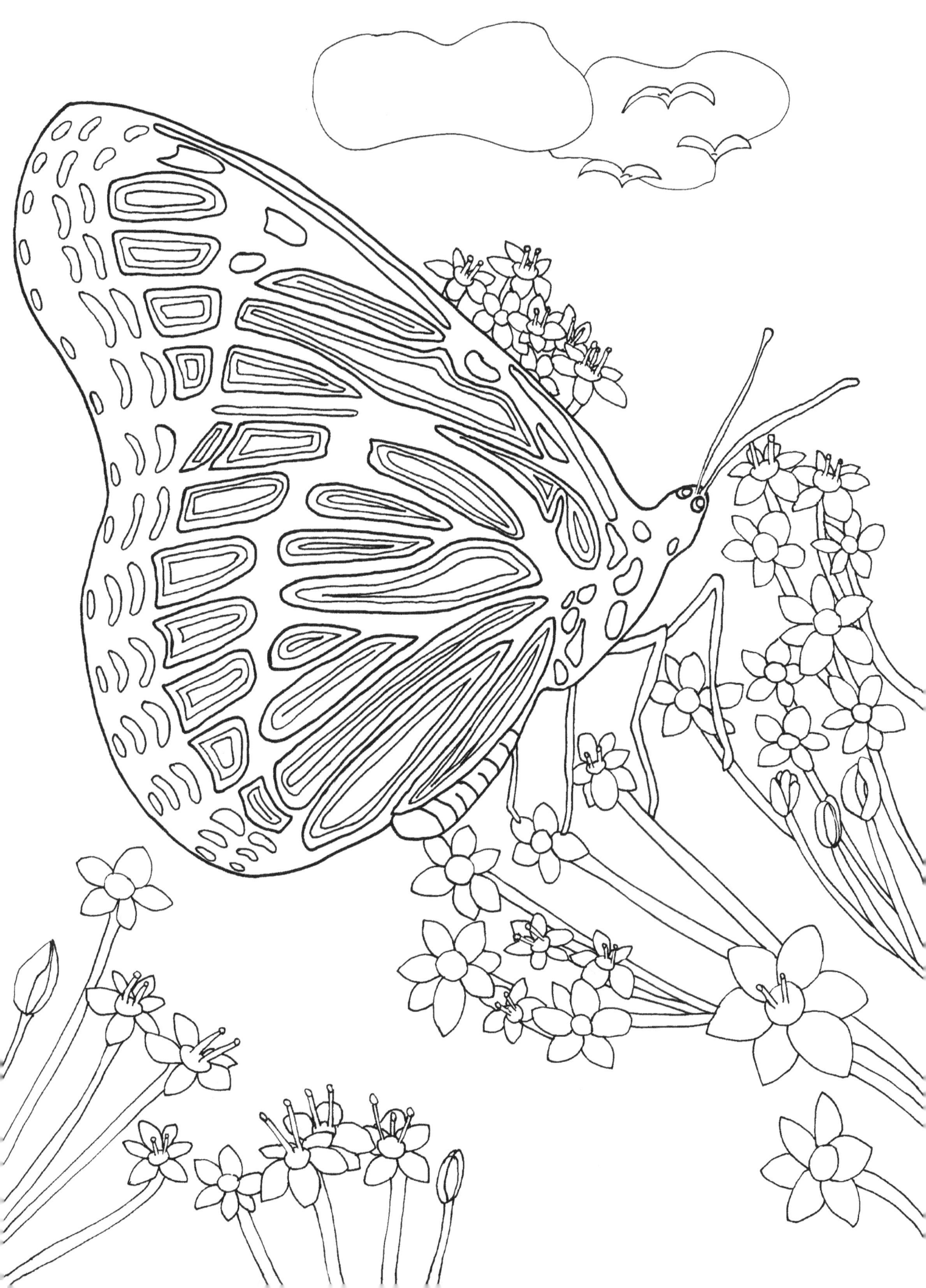

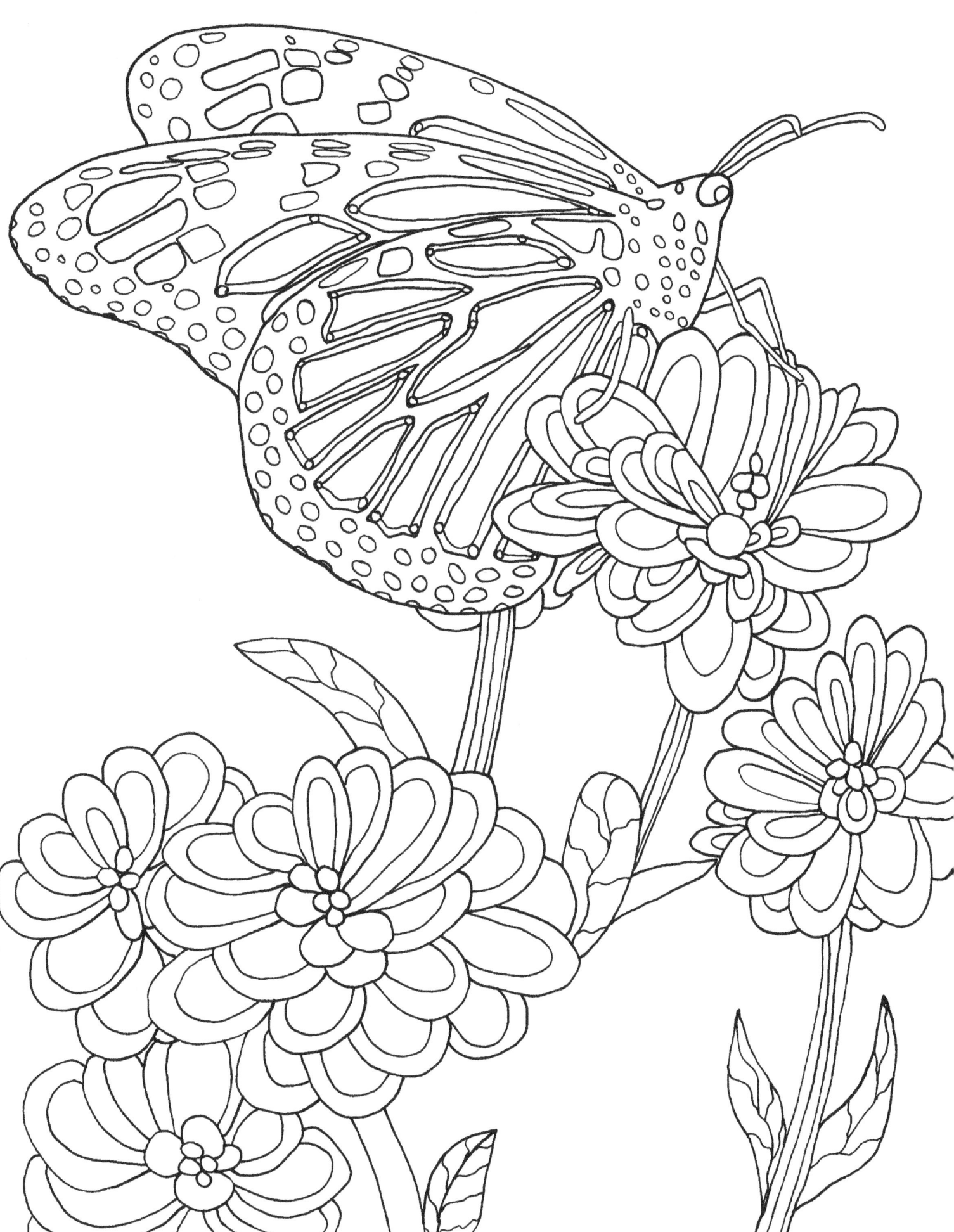

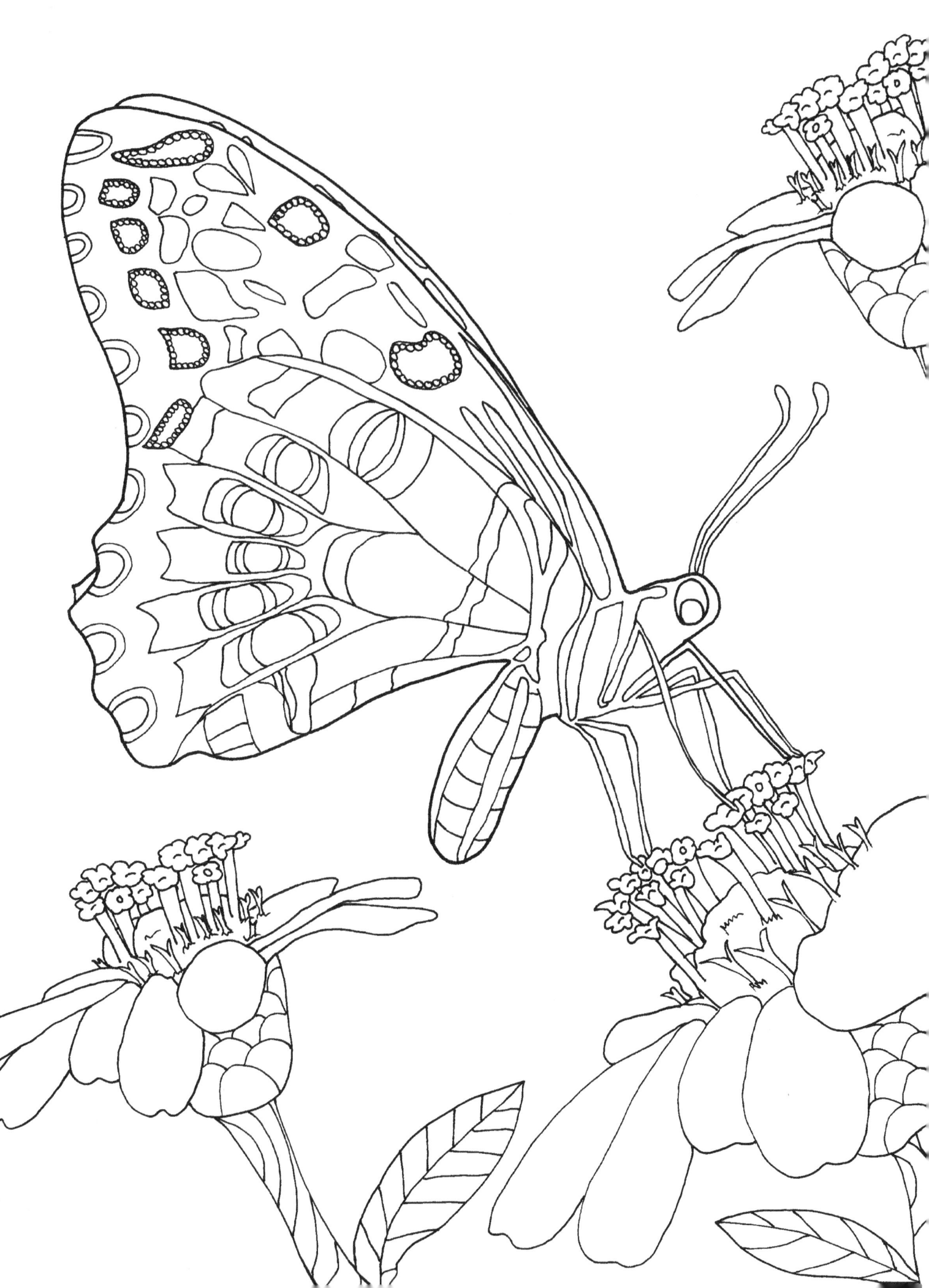

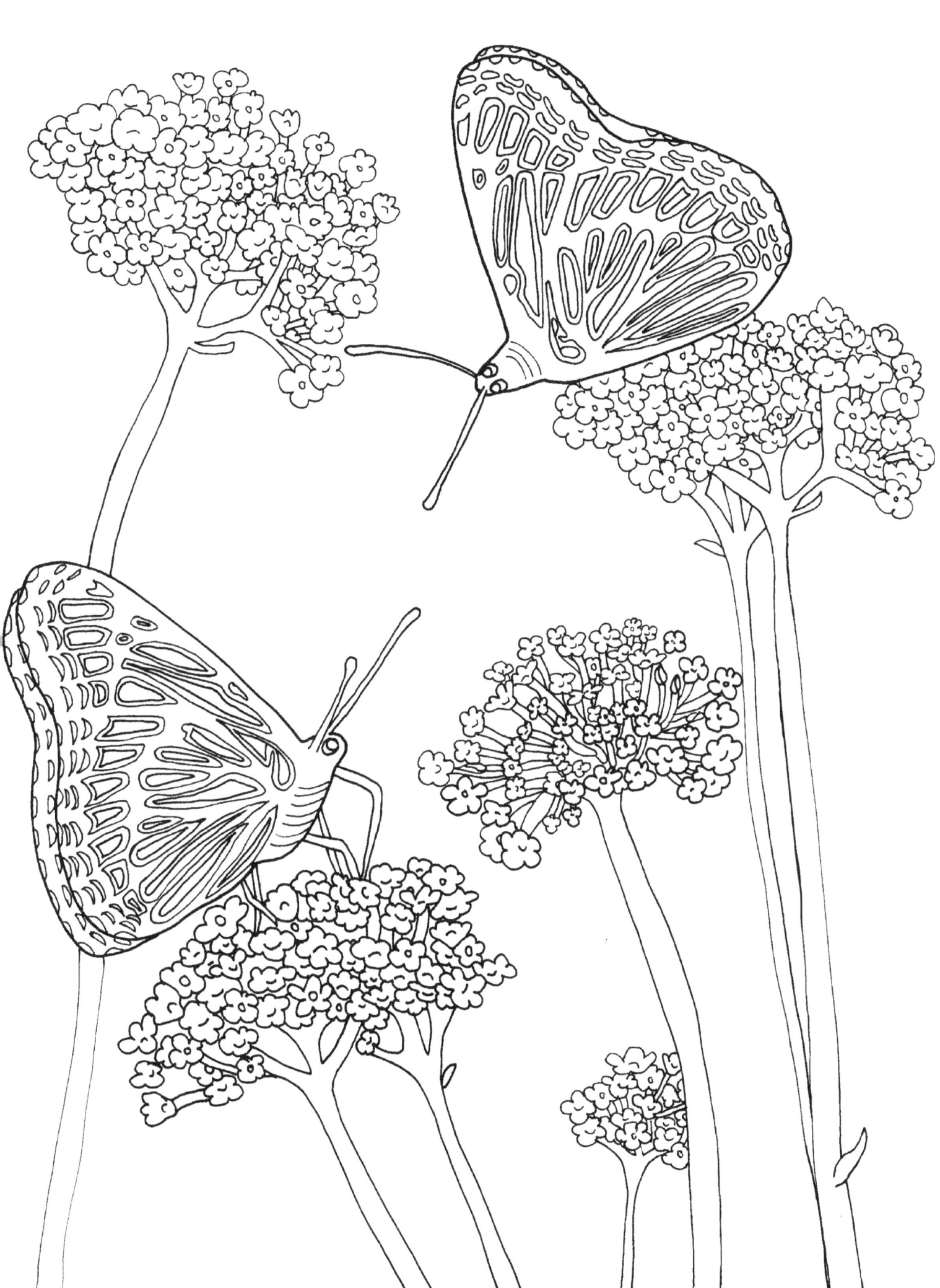

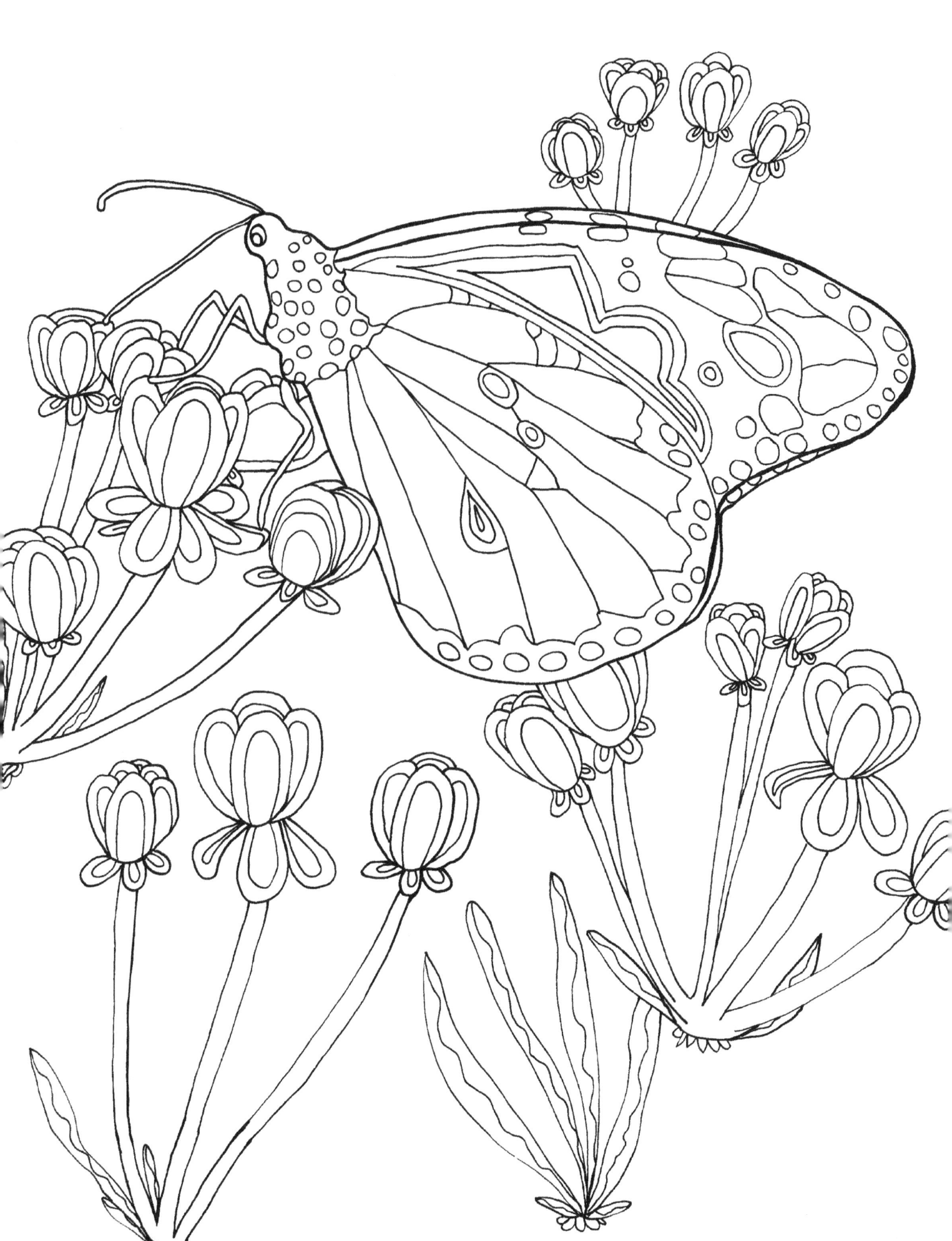

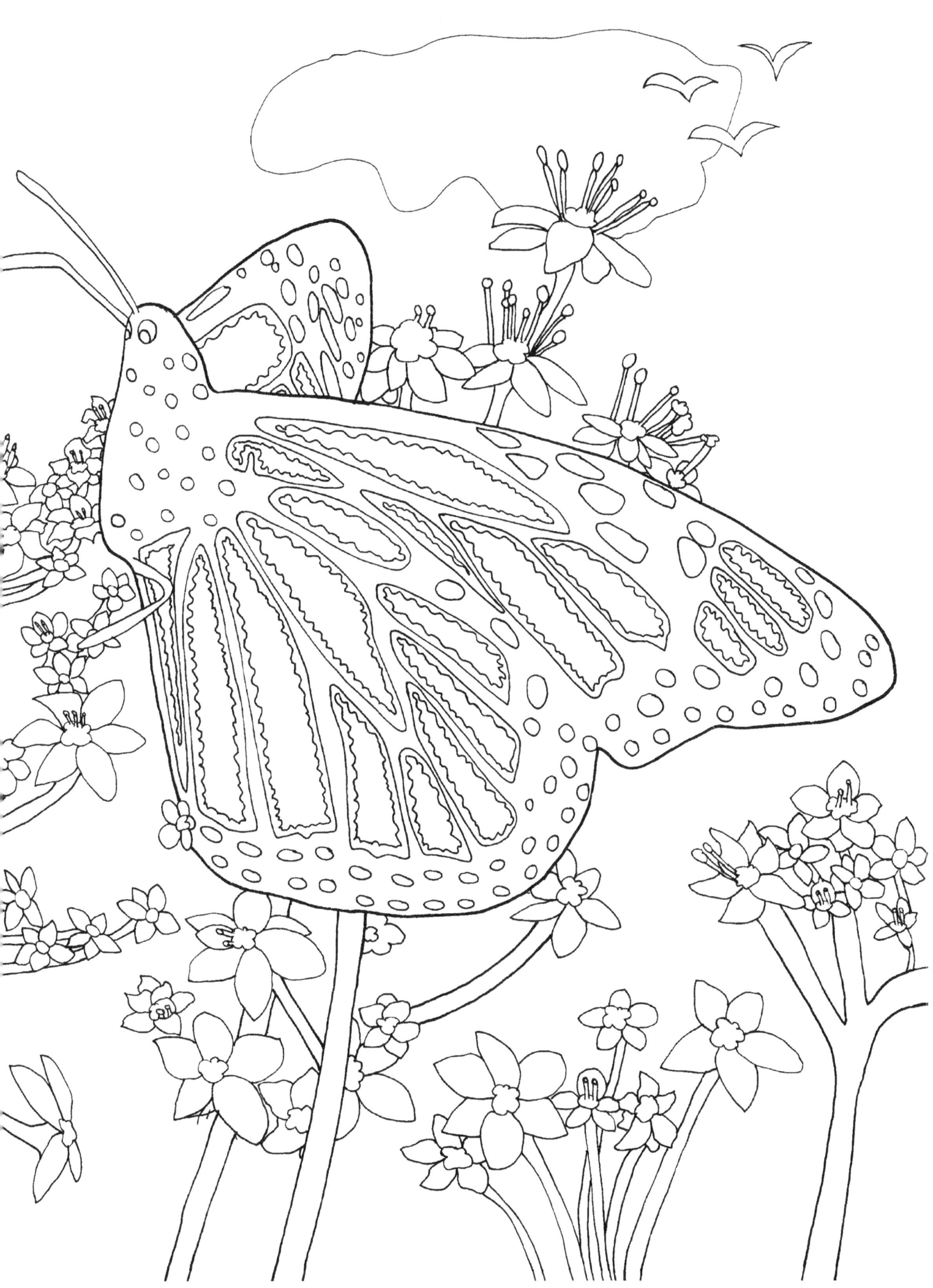

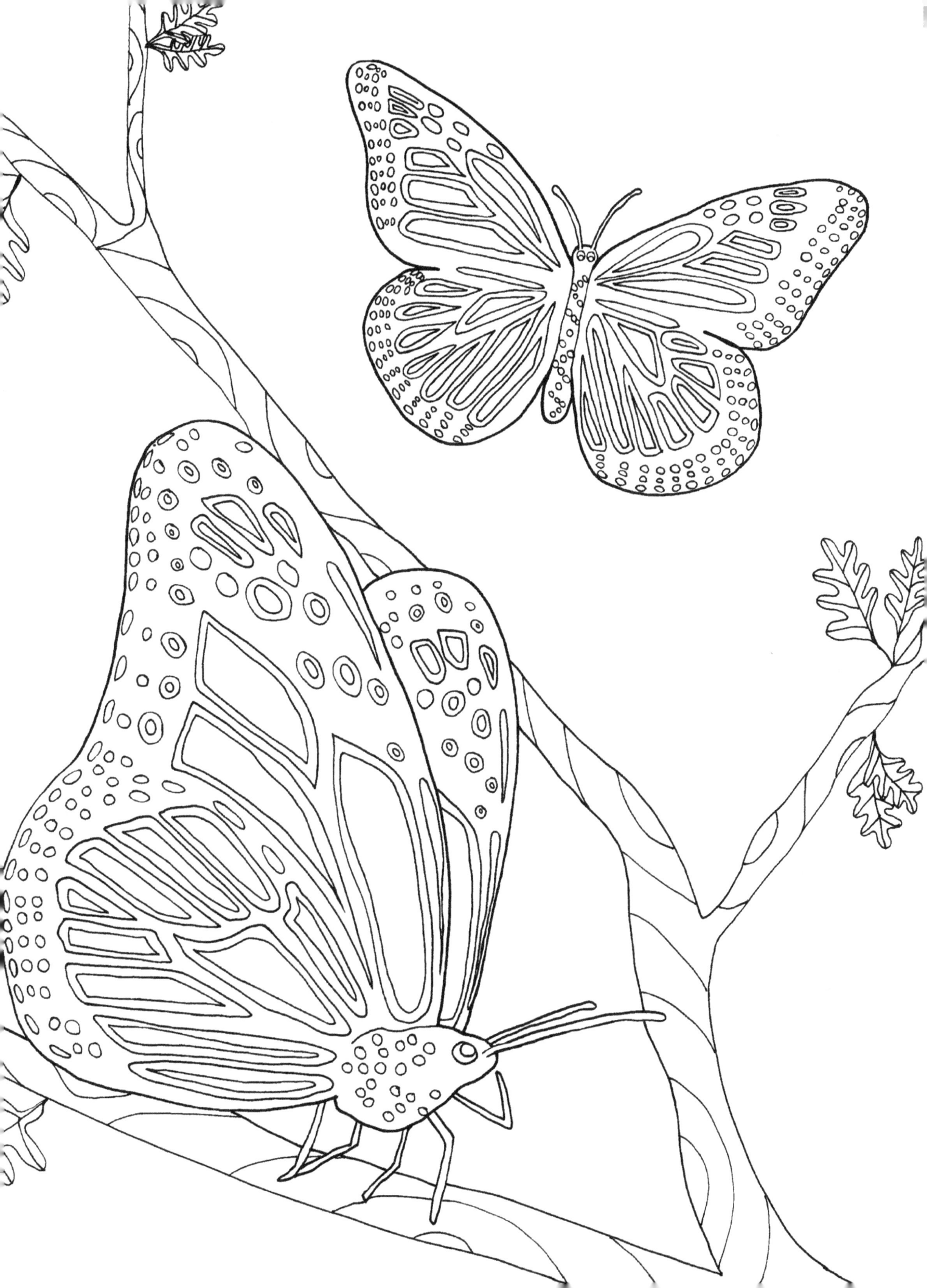

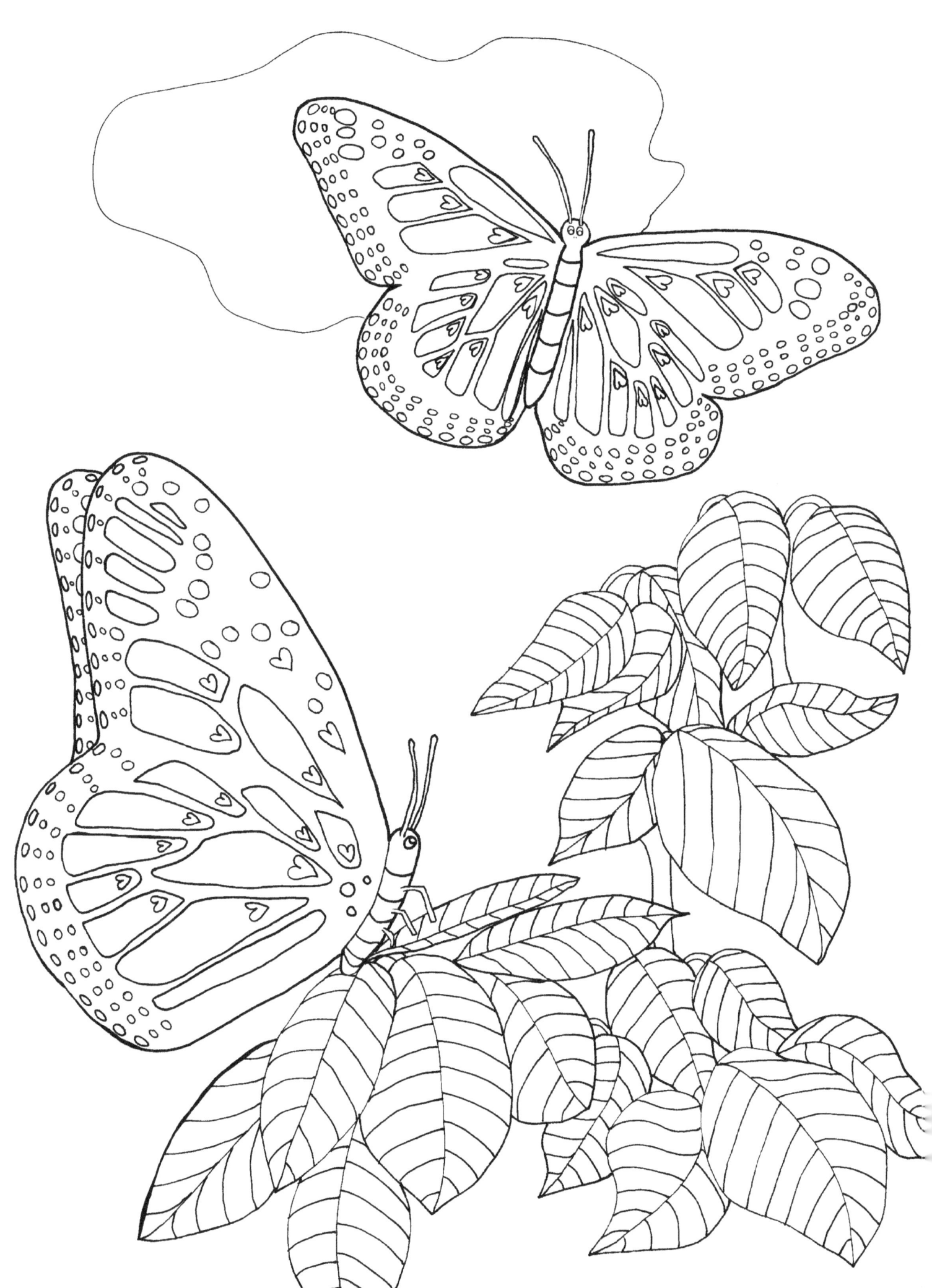

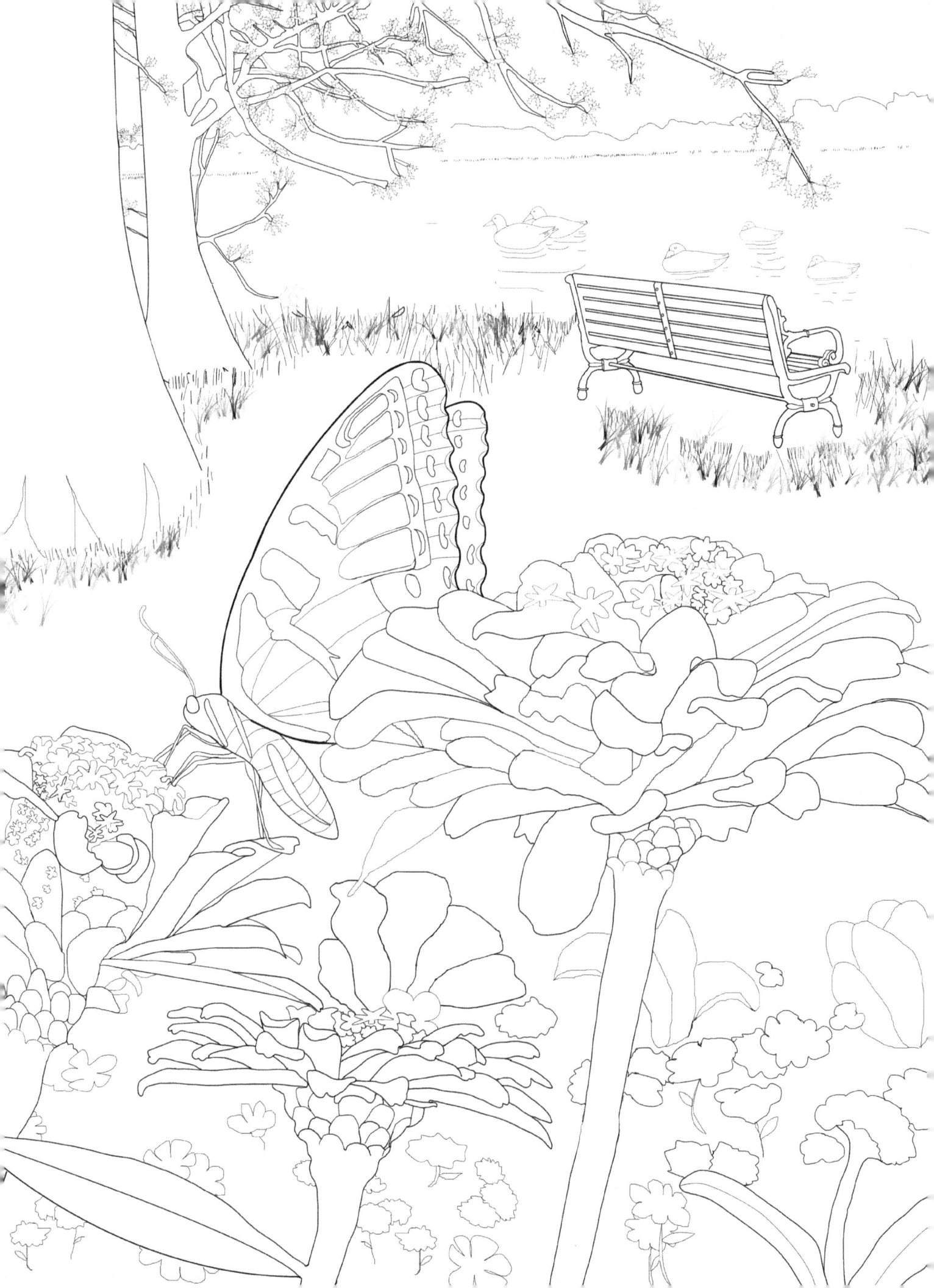

www.ingramcontent.com/pod-product-compliance
Lightning Source LLC
Chambersburg PA
CBHW080422290526
45791CB00008BA/2374

* 9 7 8 0 9 9 6 8 3 5 5 0 3 *